VIOLENCE IN SOU_____ AFRICA
A Christi_____ __t

VIOLENCE IN SOUTHERN AFRICA

A Christian Assessment

Report of a Working Party appointed by the
Department of International Affairs of
The British Council of Churches and
The Conference of British Missionary Societies

SCM PRESS LTD

334 01740 8

First published 1970
by SCM Press Ltd
56 Bloomsbury Street London WC1

© SCM Press Ltd 1970

Typeset in Great Britain by
Gloucester Typesetting Co Ltd and
printed by Whitefriars Press Ltd
Tonbridge

Contents

Because

Because my mouth is wide with laughter
And my throat is deep with song,
You do not think I suffer;
Although I have held my pain so long!

Because my mouth is wide with laughter
You do not hear my inner cry;
Because my feet are gay with dancing
You do not know, I die.

(~~Unknown, of US Negro Origin.~~)
Langston Hughes

You Tell Me to Sit Quiet

You tell me to sit quiet
When robbed of my manhood,
With nowhere to live
And nought to call my own,
Now coming, now going,
Wandering and wanting;
No life in my home
Save the drone of the beetle!
Go tell the drooping grass,
Frost bitten and pale,
Not to quicken when roused
By the warm summer rains.

> The late Dr A. C. Jordan, a South African
> (Once lecturer in African Studies, University
> of Capetown; then at University of California,
> USA; and at time of death Professor of
> African Studies at University of Wisconsin.
> Refugee out of South Africa for activity in
> the South Africa Unity Movement.)

Membership of the Working Party

The Working Party was appointed by the Department of International Affairs at its meeting on 20th/21st September 1968. The aim of the report is to help Christians in Britain, and their organizations, as they seek to form attitudes and policies towards Southern Africa.

Chairman	Philip Mason	
Rapporteur	Tom Baird	
Secretary	R. Elliott Kendall	
Membership	Arthur W. Blaxall	Ronald K. Orchard
	Kenneth R. Johnstone	Clifford J. Parsons
	Walter Makhulu	H. R. Sydenham
	Picton Mbatha	Matthew Wakatama
	Paul Oestreicher	Hugh E. Wilcox

A number of other persons, African and European, were invited to attend, either to give evidence or to express opinions.

Eleven meetings were held and an average of ten persons were present.

Foreword

All over the world there are people fiercely questioning the injustice and corruption of the societies in which they live. In the rich, and mostly white, countries they are to be found more often among the young; in the poorer, and usually not white, countries, they are widespread among the educated. There is a special resentment at injustice felt to be racial.

These people are idealists, eager for justice. Some are explicitly Christian, some actively reject Christianity; among the young, ideals are often imperfectly formulated. But rapidly growing among them is a rejection of any expectation of gradual reform, a belief that change must be complete and radical. Such change, they feel, can be achieved only by violence, and the words 'revolution' and 'violence', which to older people in Britain have connotations that are only bad, to them begin to seem good in themselves.

Those in this frame of mind are ready to support violent revolutionary movements, in Africa, in Asia, in South America, which to most professing Christians in Britain are probably objects of suspicion. Yet, in some cases at least, the active revolutionaries, too, are idealists, seeking a remedy for ills they find intolerable by the only method they can see. How should Christians in Britain judge them and their supporters here? The Department of International Affairs of the British Council of Churches at first considered asking a Working Party to report on these movements in general, but wisely decided, at any rate to start with, to limit the enquiry to revolutionary violence in Southern Africa, that is, South Africa, South-West Africa, Rhodesia, Angola and Mozambique. This is the resulting report.

The audience to whom it is directed is British. It seeks to illuminate the thinking of British Christians about revolutionary violence. It does *not* seek to provide a blueprint for dealing with the problems of Southern Africa. These points can hardly be too strongly emphasized.

It may be asked why attention should once again be directed to Southern Africa, when there are so many injustices and miseries all over the world. The reasons, set out more fully in the Report, are, first, that we in Britain have a special responsibility for Southern Africa, because of our long political association, our trade ties, financial investment, and defence agreement, because of involvement in the mission field, and special relations with churches in Southern Africa, because of our association with South African universities. Nor is this old history; throughout the Third World we are seen today as tacitly supporting South Africa. Secondly, we believe that the South African régime denies the dignity which human beings ought to possess more explicitly than any other authoritarian régime and claims that it is thereby defending Christian principle. It is a Christian responsibility to refute this claim.

The Report, we hope, speaks for itself. It is unanimous. There were inevitably many differences of emphasis; almost every member at some point agreed to make concessions to the majority about the wording of some passage. But in the main argument all the participants concurred, as did most of those who came only for certain sessions. It is the work of several hands, as will be apparent to a careful reader. Some editing has been carried out in order to make the different contributions read consecutively, but this has not, it is hoped, been carried so far as to spoil the spontaneity of individual contributions.

Introduction

In South Africa a man and his wife who have been living together happily for years may be forcibly separated by the operation of the law; the wife and children may be sent back to her birthplace while he is working in Johannesburg, or he may suddenly be removed from South Africa as a 'foreign native'. In 1965/66, over a thousand Africans were arrested each day for not carrying the right documents and were fined, usually after one or two nights in the cells. In his work, in his home, in his daily movement, an African is subject to sharp personal restriction.

In Rhodesia education for black and white is separate, and the amount spent on a white child is more than ten times as much as that spent on a black child. Yet the average income of white people is ten times that of black; in 1964 the figures were £1,241 compared to £121. The latest land legislation in Rhodesia makes forty-four million acres available for the use of Europeans, leaving forty-four million acres for Africans. The population figures are roughly 220,000 Europeans and four and a half million Africans. On average this means one hundred and eighty acres for each European and ten acres for each African.

It is injustices of this kind – and we shall mention many more – that have caused the majority of Africans in these two countries to regard the government as their enemy – an enemy which is holding them in subjection by the systematic use of force and to which the only answer they can see is revolutionary violence. Peaceful protest has been tried in vain. Hopes of gradual improvement have been destroyed, as new laws have one by one been passed to end the few liberties that once existed for Africans.

Every government makes use of force and some use of force is legitimate when the people of the state regard the government as *theirs*. But when a majority regard the government as alien, a point may be reached when the restraining force must be regarded as unjust and violent. In Mozambique, Angola, South-West Africa, Rhodesia and South Africa, with many differences, there is one factor in common. The belief is widespread among Africans that they are governed by an authority to which they have not consented and which enforces its will unjustly and by violence. For that violence we in Britain cannot disclaim at least some responsibility so long as Portugal and South Africa are our allies, so long as Saracen armoured cars bought from Britain still patrol the streets of South Africa, so long as Buccaneer aircraft contribute to the military strength which enables South Africa to defy world opinion.

This is the situation which this book seeks to discuss; this is the background to revolutionary activities in Angola and Mozambique and to raids into Rhodesia. What should be the attitude of a Christian to such a situation? One thing at least is essential if he is to make a sound and charitable judgment; he must understand something of what is happening and why Africans regard it as they do.

Southern Africa

It is important to realize not only the poignancy and urgency but also the scale of events in Southern Africa. This vast area of two million square miles consists of eight territories ranging in size from Angola and South Africa (each of which is five times the size of the United Kingdom) to the tiny states of Lesotho and Swaziland (the size of Wales and Yorkshire respectively). The full list of countries involved is as follows: South Africa, South-West Africa (Namibia), Angola, Mozambique, Rhodesia, Botswana, Lesotho and Swaziland.[1]

It is with the first five countries in this list that we shall be most concerned, for it is in these territories that the government is felt by most of the population to be alien and that men and women live in conditions of gross indignity.

South Africa, South-West Africa, Angola, Mozambique and Rhodesia contain thirty-five million people.[2] The vast majority (more than 85%) of the inhabitants are non-whites. Thirty-one million people are being ruled by white minorities. They have no say in their government, which they believe is conducted for the benefit of the minority. They are denied the most elementary of human rights. The political and social dangers of the situation in Southern Africa cannot be properly assessed until the plight of these people is understood.[3]

Later in this report we shall be considering in more detail the moral and political significance of the guerrilla movements and their efforts to liberate the people of Southern Africa by violence.

[1] See map on p. 118.
[2] 95% of the population of the whole of Southern Africa is found in these five territories.
[3] The figures quoted in this Report are, wherever possible, from official publications. They are therefore not always up to date. But more recent, if also more arguable figures, do not suggest any improvement.

At this stage we wish to emphasize the extent to which force instead of consent is being used by the governments concerned, not simply as a last resort kept in reserve, but as a normal method of maintaining control. Since this control is used to maintain the economic and political privilege of the white minority, it is seen by the black majority as unjust. To them, the military and police action of the state is violence, in no way more justifiable than any violence that might be used to overthrow the state.

Although there are variations in the five territories, the main elements of white domination and black repression are recognizably similar:

(a) refusal of the franchise, that is, of the right to vote in national elections;

(b) denial of the freedom to live and work in the place of one's choice, often involving the break-up of families;

(c) inequalities of wages and conditions of work;

(d) denial of the right to marry the person of one's choice;

(e) denial of the right to free movement within the country;

(f) denial of the right of free speech and freedom to meet;

(g) severe restrictions on educational opportunities;

(h) constant liability to arrest, and continual exposure to the arbitrary action of the police.

These factors are significantly present in all the five territories being considered in Southern Africa, to a greater or lesser degree. These social conditions add up to a continual experience of indignity and frustration. There are many who have resisted these restrictions and are consequently in prison or exile.[4] They are representative of the millions living as second-class citizens

[4] In the Republic of South Africa, the latest official figure that is available for political prisoners is for December 1967. There were then 1,335 prisoners convicted under the state security laws and their offences ranged from placing a bomb in the offices of the 'Bantu Administration' offices, to writing in chalk on a wall 'apartheid out'. The number of detainees held in solitary confinement, incommunicado, under the Terrorism Act and the '180-day law' is not known as only the Minister of Justice may give the number if he so wishes, and if he does not wish to do so no one can find out. It is known that fourteen such detainees have died while in detention.

Forty-six Africans from South-West Africa are serving sentences of from five years to life imprisonment for offences under the state security laws. In Rhodesia, the Minister of Law and Order stated on 17th April, 1969 that there were 211 persons in restriction and 142 in detention. They have not been charged, tried, or convicted but are held for their political views.

in Southern Africa who are silent because they are controlled by
government violence or the fear of it.

We cannot accept the view that this is none of our concern.
Britain has had, and continues to have, strong historic, cultural
and economic links with this area of Africa. Towards Rhodesia
Britain has a special responsibility, internationally recognized,
and asserted at the United Nations by successive British governments. Commercial, industrial and financial relations between
South Africa and Britain should not be regarded in isolation
from considerations of compassion and humanity which we, as
Christians, share with many humanists and agnostics. But, as
Christians, we must further denounce as manifestly untrue the
pretence that the social and political conditions we are describ-
ing are a 'defence of Christian civilization'.

The Christian faith challenges us to strive for the worth and
dignity of every human being, and to seek to embody justice and
love in social structures. We cannot escape a profound concern
for *caritas* or love, and for justice.

It may perplex or distress some people who have visited
Southern Africa that we write here in such tragic language of the
miseries of many people there. There are visitors from Europe
and America who visit Southern Africa as tourists, or briefly on
business, and claim that the majority of Africans in South Africa,
Rhodesia and other territories are cheerful and satisfied. More-
over, visitors are often impressed by the scale and speed of industrial development, by the discipline and order of society, and by
the comfort and affluence which they are able briefly to share.

There are also some whose visits are less fleeting and whose
business and social relations with the government, with firms
and with individuals are intimate and of long standing. In some
cases it may be that their interest is limited to business; in almost all it is inevitable from the nature of the situation that they
hear only the point of view of the ruling group.

Visitors who make only a short stay in Southern Africa, who
have not studied its history, or who have talked only to whites of
the ruling group, need to reflect on the following considerations:

The governments concerned discourage visitors from seeing
the worst aspects of society. It is only with great difficulty that

the occasional visitor can make any contact with African communities in the tribal reserves of Rhodesia, Mozambique or South Africa, or indeed in the urban areas. Similarly, police control and victimization are not often witnessed by outsiders and the majority of white people, even of those who live in Southern Africa, know little about the life of African communities;

non-white people have to come to terms with the unchanging conditions of their life as oppressed peoples. If they display a façade of cheerfulness and tolerance under grave indignities, it does not mean that they do not suffer;

casual contact between a visitor from outside and a member of the subject group within an authoritarian regime can seldom be of more than limited value. People have to be careful what they say when they live in a society riddled with espionage and overshadowed by harsh legislation, by arrest without warrant and by detention without trial. They are reluctant to explain their real feelings and attitudes to strangers;

what the casual visitor learns from personal observation needs to be checked against background knowledge, both of Southern African history and of the contemporary situation. He needs to understand, for example, the complexity and pervasiveness of discriminatory legislation; the system of migrant labour from within South Africa and from neighbouring territories for South African industry; the working of the Pass Laws and of the Group Areas Act. Several hundred thousand Africans come to work in the mines, accepting separation for years from home and family, and living in highly artificial conditions. A visitor should try to understand the social consequences of this system.

Having stressed the dangers of a superficial judgment, the Working Party must present its own credentials. For some of us, these territories are home; this is where we were born and brought up; here are the places and the people we love. For us it is a heavy and continual burden that our own societies are dark with hostility and suppression of freedom. Other members of the Working Party, though they belong to the United Kingdom, have lived for many years in one or other of these territories and have witnessed with sadness the steady growth of tyranny. The small minority who cannot claim long residence have for many years given time to specialized study and travel.

2

The Five Territories
A Social and Historical Study

The territories of Southern Africa vary not only in size but in racial composition and in density of population.[1]

Country	Area (in square miles)	Total Population	Proportion of whites in total population
S. Africa	471,445	18,733,000	1 in 5
S.W. Africa	318,099	537,261	1 in 7
Angola	481,352	4,833,000	1 in 21
Mozambique	297,731	6,480,000	1 in 50
Rhodesia	150,333	4,460,000	1 in 20
Botswana	220,236	543,105	1 in 140
Lesotho	11,716	975,000	1 in 487
Swaziland	6,705	374,571	1 in 47

It is with the first five that we are concerned. The last three territories were formerly governed by the British High Commissioner in South Africa and were known as the High Commission Territories. All three have recently gained their independence within the Commonwealth on the basis of majority rule. Thus they are not ruled by a racially alien minority and although their problems, which are considerable, are enhanced by their dependence on South Africa and Mozambique, their affairs are only incidental to this Report.

(i) *South Africa*

South Africa is incomparably the most powerful country in the area. Not only in terms of population but economically, politically and militarily she holds the dominant position in Southern

[1] Figures given are from Penguin *Africa Handbook*, 1969. Later official estimates of population in South Africa are as follows:

(June 1969)	Whites	3,700,000	Coloured 1,900,000
	Africans	13,300,000	Asians 500,000
Total: 19,400,000.			

Africa. The history of white occupation goes back to the middle
of the seventeenth century. For many centuries before, Hottentots and Bushmen had lived in the southern part of Africa.
Bantu-speaking Africans (from central and north-east Africa)
had migrated south and these three groups were already present
when the first colonists from Europe settled at the Cape in 1652,
though the colonists did not at first meet the Bantu-speakers.
Some small tribes were nomadic, but the vast majority were living in settled communities. It was not an empty unpopulated
country. The survival of Bushmen and Hottentots was threat-
ened by Bantu-speaking Africans[2] and Europeans, but the major
tension for the future lay between the two last named groups.

The first immigrants were from the Netherlands, but before
the end of the seventeenth century French and German Protestant settlers had joined them. The situation was further compli-
cated by a new challenge to the predominantly Dutch settler
community, when in 1795, during the Napoleonic Wars, the
British annexed the Cape. It was handed back to the Dutch in
1803, but the British resumed control in 1806. This was the
beginning of a British presence in South Africa which ended
when she became a Republic and left the Commonwealth.

The British brought new ideas of government and of the relation between employer and servant, but it would be a mistake to
picture British immigrants purveying liberal ideas to reluctant
Boers. The situation was more complex, and it would be nearer
the truth to think of liberal ideas originating in Britain at one
end of a scale at the other extreme of which were the ideas of the
most rigid and isolated Afrikaner groups on the advancing frontier. There were many intermediate positions. There was indeed
considerable cultural antagonism between the two groups, but
this antagonism obscured and overlay the essential South
African problem, the relation between Europeans and Africans.
On this there were divergent views, often, though not necessarily, dividing British and Afrikaner, but there were occasions
when the bond uniting all the white settlers was stronger than
that between the British settlers and the British government.
The Dutch had early introduced slaves from West and East

2 Bushmen were hunters, Hottentots pastoralists; they were therefore sparse
populations incapable of the sustained resistance of the agricultural Bantu-
speakers.

Africa, and from Batavia, and all the settler-groups soon grew accustomed to owning slaves. The movement originating in Britain to emancipate the slaves was resented by many of the settlers of the Cape Colony; the abolition of the Slave Trade in 1807 and the ending of slavery itself in British-held territories in 1834 were welcome to few. There were difficulties over the way in which compensation was arranged, and the tensions created were one of the causes of the Afrikaner trek to the north. The trek, however, was more an attempt to escape from the ideas of the British government than from fellow settlers of British speech. The trekkers settled in two northern areas, the Orange Free State (as it was later called) and the Transvaal, where their racial attitudes were symbolized by the Orange Free State constitution, the 'Grondwet', of 1854 which stated: 'The people (whites) will permit no equality between White and Black in either Church or State'. Thus from the time of the Great Trek onwards those who followed this mainly Afrikaner tradition turned their faces away from the liberal traditions coming from Europe. They sought to keep themselves wholly apart from the African people in their social and political life, although at the same time they relied on African labour.

The Cape Colony, on the other hand, from 1854, possessed a constitution which made no legal distinctions on grounds of race. It was a well-known Cape saying that the law was 'colour blind'. The franchise was restricted, as it was at this time in England, to the male sex and to those with fixed standards of property and education. These standards admitted very few Africans, but some Africans did have the vote and it was possible for liberals to believe that the racial imbalance would gradually be cured. In the discussions leading up to the Act of Union (1910), one of the points of difference was the comparatively liberal spirit of the Cape. This was shared by many of Dutch and Huguenot extraction, and it is as near the truth to think of a contrast between the Cape and the Transvaal as of one between British and Dutch.

Representatives of Great Britain, like those of the Cape, wished to see Cape liberalism embodied in the Act of Union, those of the Transvaal and the Orange Free State were resolute in opposition. The British gave way, determined to be generous to the

Afrikaner, even at the expense of the African; it was believed in Whitehall that, with the spread of education and the gradual development of industry and communications, more liberal views would prevail. But this was illusion; the reverse has proved to be the case. For the next fifty years the political pendulum swung to and fro between the extreme Afrikaner nationalist position and the more moderate stance represented by the United Party. But even when the United Party was in power it seldom exercised itself on behalf of the underprivileged, and political power remained firmly in the hands of the white minority. The mainly British United Party showed no more enthusiasm than the Nationalists for an extension of the franchise. So much for the white side of the story.

On the African side, the Hottentots were scattered or reduced to servitude. For the Bantu-speakers, however, the picture is one of long and bitter resistance. It seems that the Cape colonists encountered Bantu-speaking Africans for the first time near the Fish River in the Eastern Cape about 1750: this was the first of many fierce engagements that recurred for more than a century in what are now known as the 'Kaffir Wars'. (Africans regard this as a derogatory term, and speak of African Wars of Resistance, or Liberation.) The white invasion from the Cape and the gradual extension of white supremacy over the whole area of what is now the Republic were indeed physically resisted by the African people with all the force available to them.

During the eighteenth century the boundary between the European settler in the Eastern Cape and the African people was well understood, although there were trading connections and occasionally small raids for cattle from both sides. In 1778, the Governor marked the boundary with beacons and forbade white people to cross.

Towards the end of the eighteenth century the first major clashes took place between the white colonists on the frontier of the Cape and the Bantu-speaking peoples to the east and northeast. The root of the conflict lay in the desire for the control and use of land.

On the eastern frontiers of the Cape, in the course of a century of warfare, the Xhosa and related peoples put up surely one of

the most sustained displays of resistance to white control anywhere in Africa. The strength and constancy of their resistance
is evidenced today by the fact that only part of the area was ap-
propriated, and the large amount of land which remained in their
possession is now the 'Bantustan' of the Transkei.

Reluctantly, Cape Governments assumed responsibility for
their frontiersmen. They tried to maintain order between
groups competing for hunting and grazing lands, and to stop
raiding from both sides for cattle. The Xhosa, for their part,
fought bitterly to retain their land and independence, and between six and nine wars followed over a hundred years – the
number depends on the point at which raiding and retaliation
may be termed war. During this time the frontier moved east-
ward and the whites, who were better armed (since they traded
with the outside world) and members of an organized state,
conquered a people who were much more numerous, but ill-
armed, and without any central authority.[3]

Each year, on 16th December, the celebration by Afrikaners
of the Day of the Covenant, recalls the battle at Blood River, in
which Zulu resistance to Boer expansion was overcome, leaving
three thousand Zulus dead.

The desire for land was for the Afrikaner at the root of the
armed struggle; for his was a civilization of pastoralists. The
Afrikaner felt that every male was entitled to a large area of land
for farming. The English community also included a farming
population, but the majority of English were engaged in trade
and administration. Ownership of land by white farmers, however, was in direct conflict with the interests of African tribal
pastoralists, with their herds and shifting cultivation. There was
consequently a bitter fight for possession of the soil.

In 1820 4,000 British settlers were established west of the
Fish River. War with the Xhosa broke out fourteen years later
and recurred three times within the next thirty years.

The Xhosa lost the greater part of their land to the whites.
Twelve thousand Xhosa warriors crossed the Fish in 1834 but
they were defeated within five months.

[3] *The Oxford History of South Africa*, Vol. 1, 1969, pp. 240–1, 252.

The Xhosa were fighting not primarily for booty but for survival as an independent people.[4]

In 1851 the Xhosa again attacked and fought a bitter war. The
year 1878 witnessed a war with the Gcaleka, who were attempting to regain land which had been taken from them.

Armed resistance of this kind continued until the twentieth
century. The Zulu War of 1879, for example, began with the
complete destruction of a force of British regular troops by a
Zulu impi. But, except for the High Commission Territories,
which became Protectorates, the outcome for the Bantu-speaking
Africans was in general conquest and loss of land; the tribal areas
which remained became smaller and smaller. Shortage of land
and the need to pay taxes forced the young men into the towns
to get work, and as the century progressed, armed resistance became on the whole less frequent. It began to look as though the
Africans would become simply a menial class at the bottom of
the social scale in a new state which was already developing on
capitalist lines in the manner familiar in Europe and America.
In the Cape Province, this fate had already overtaken the
'Coloured', that is, the people of mixed blood, many of them
descendants of the former slaves. The Hottentots as organized
tribes had ceased to exist; would the same happen to Bantu-
speakers?

By the turn of the century, South Africa, although still a predominantly agricultural country, was being radically changed
economically by the exploitation of diamond, gold and other
mineral resources. Demand for African labour became more in-
tense and thousands were brought from the rural areas into the
growing townships. The industrial centres saw the uncontrolled
growth of shanty-towns; industry and local government sought
to house the workers in labour compounds. This development
has taken place at a time of great population growth, so that today
one African worker residential area may contain half-a-million
people. In the first decades of this century, a young African,
whose grandfather half a century or so earlier would have been
fighting on the frontier against white expansion, was compelled

[4] *The Oxford History of South Africa*, Vol. 1, 1969, pp. 240–1, 249.

instead to adapt himself to life in an industrial environment as a migrant worker.

Something not altogether unlike this happened in nineteenth-century Britain also. But in South Africa the uprooting was more complete because it involved a complete change of culture. Further, and far more significantly, legal steps were taken to preserve the privileges of the rich and to prevent any narrowing of the gap between rich and poor. Urban life for the African worker has brought increasingly strict control. For Africans – but not for whites, who are free – the law regulates exactly where a man may live, where he may eat, work, sit; whom he may marry; what, when and where he may drink. All these regulations – which will be described in detail in chapter 3 – put him at the mercy of the police.

With some notable exceptions, the traditional African leaders, the Chiefs, had failed to prevent white conquest, either by physical resistance or by diplomacy. In their place a new type of African leader emerged with a background of mission school and university. Liberal and Christian African leaders attempted to work within the new political system, and to develop African education, but they did not relinquish the ultimate objective of achieving emancipation for their people.

The creation of the Union of South Africa in 1910 was against the will of the African people, and neither secured their rights as they understood them, nor held out any likelihood of their political aspirations being realized. The South African Native National Congress[5] was formed as a response to the imposition of Union. Its founder spoke of the need to overcome tribal divisions and rivalries, so that Africans could present a united front against the new white South African government. In 1913 Africans protested strongly against the passing of the Native Land Act which reserved nearly 90% of the country for the use of the white population. Petitions and deputations to the South African and British governments were unsuccessful.

Until the first world war, African protest was limited to pass-burning demonstrations or local strikes. During the period between the wars, especially in times of economic depression, Africans protested against their working conditions and treat-

[5] Later its name was changed to African National Congress.

ment. Occasionally there were outbreaks of mob violence, such as the burning of a police van at Vereeniging and the murder of its occupants. The immediate cause of most disruption was the 'pass' – to be carried at all times and to be produced on demand to prove that the holder is employed, and therefore entitled to be present in a particular area. Workers expressed their attitudes in strikes and boycotts. At a different level the African National Congress (ANC) passed resolutions and presented petitions, such as those against the Hertzog Bills of 1936, the main purport of which was to disfranchise Africans in the Cape Province.

In the 'thirties some leading Africans were of the opinion that 'we can no longer loyally serve and be subject to a government which has openly disowned us and told us in brutal language that we can never, never be free'.

During the war the much-publicized Allied War Aims reached the remotest corners of South Africa and ordinary people read of self-determination, freedom and equality. Many Africans served with armies overseas. Those from other territories might be combatants but, if they came from South Africa, neither African nor coloured volunteers were allowed to bear arms. Later they were informed that they were not entitled to ex-soldiers' pensions because 'they never bore arms for South Africa'.

The present leaders of bodies like the ANC grew up in such experiences, and at the conclusion of hostilities began to talk of social and political equality. The demands of post-war African leaders were no longer for a simple sharing in some of the features of South African life, but for radical changes which would bring equality. In 1946 Parliament ignored a petition asking for the repeal of repressive legislation.

In 1948 the Nationalist Party came to power in South Africa, in a narrow but momentous victory, pledged to implement a policy of Apartheid.[6] Within five years the following legislation was passed and became effective: The Prohibition of Mixed Marriages Act, The Immorality Amendment Act, The Suppression of Communism Act, The Population Registration Act, The Separate Representation of Voters Act, The Bantu Education

---

[6] White reaction to claims generally in line with, and often more moderate than, those being made throughout the continent.

Act, The Bantu[7] Persons Abolition of Passes and Co-ordination
of Documents Act, The Native[7] Labour Settlement of Disputes
Act, The Asiatic Land Tenure Amendment Act, The Asiatic
Laws Amendment Act, The Prevention of Illegal Squatting
Act, The Native Laws Amendment Act, The Native Building
Workers Act, The Unemployment Insurance Amendment Act,
The Group Areas Act, The Public Safety Act, The Bantu
Authorities Act, The Native Labour Act, The Criminal Law
Amendment Act. Under these laws, African, Coloured[7] and
Asian people are placed in completely separate categories from
white South Africans, are deprived of whatever voting rights
they may have had, are restricted in areas of residence and choice
of profession, prevented from competing for various forms of
employment or striking to better their economic position or joining racially-mixed trade unions. Africans have become aliens in
the industrial areas of their own country.

It was these laws which made it clear to Africans that there
was no hope of gradual improvement of their lot. On the contrary the ruling party was determined to keep them in subjection
for as long as it possibly could. (The operation of these laws will
be described in detail in chapter 3.)

The reaction of the ANC was to call for civil disobedience and
industrial strikes. A national passive resistance movement was
called in 1952 in the course of which 8,000 people volunteered
to offer themselves for arrest. The government response was repressive: the Criminal Laws Amendment Act and the Public
Safety Act contained extremely severe penalties for anyone found
guilty of breaking a law by way of protest, or inciting anyone else
to do so; these included not only heavy fines but flogging or
imprisonment or both.

Thus from the closing decades of the nineteenth century efforts
were made by African, Asian and Coloured people to gain political rights. The emphasis was placed on political organization,
the education of leaders and on passive resistance by both men
and women. But no progress was made towards the objective and
latterly it has receded. After the second world war the African
National Congress and other bodies were very active, but each

---

[7] 'Coloured' means people of mixed racial parentage or ancestry. The words
'Bantu' and 'Native' are interchangeable in meaning.

passing year made the task more difficult. From 1948 onwards the doctrine of 'separate development' has explicitly guided the government of South Africa, and under the premiership of Malan, Strijdom, Verwoerd and Vorster, segregation has become increasingly rigid and white privilege even more sacrosanct.

In 1950 the Population Registration Act established a Racial Register; everyone from the age of sixteen must now by law carry an identity card declaring his race – European, African or Coloured (including Asians). It can hardly be imagined how much anguish has been caused by this law. As a report to the United Nations expresses it:

> A person's racial classification is of the utmost importance to him, for it decides, *inter alia*, where he may live, how he may live, what work he may do, what sort of education he will receive, what political rights he will have, if any, whom he may marry, the extent of the social, cultural and recreational facilities open to him, and generally, the extent of his freedom of action and movement.[8]

Even these words do not disclose the personal distress and family division that the Register causes. By this Act a person whose natural parents have both been classified in the same racial group is classified in that group. If one parent is classified as 'White' and the other as 'Coloured', or 'Bantu', that person is classified as 'Coloured'. If one parent is 'Coloured' and the other 'Bantu', the person is classified as 'Bantu'. Social down-grading based on race has caused such acute suffering that the victims have sometimes committed suicide. Through reclassification, married people may find their marriage illegal and be liable to prosecution under the Immorality Act.

It was in the 'fifties that the concept of 'Bantustans' was clarified. Already in 1913, by the Native Land Act, Africans were prohibited from acquiring freehold property from other races. Protests, petitions and deputations to Pretoria and London were of no avail. The restrictions were further tightened in 1936 by the Native Trust and Land Act, which fixed the extent of land for the African population at 13% of the whole. Then in 1959 the

---

[8] *Apartheid and Racial Discrimination in Southern Africa*, United Nations, 1968, p. 6.

zoning took place of eight areas within this 13% as African
'homelands' or 'Bantustans'. According to the doctrine of
separate development, Africans are only to consider themselves
at home within these areas. Anywhere else they are migrant
workers without rights. These 'homelands' are scattered about
the country and vary immensely in area. Often the land is poor
and unproductive. Generally there is over-population and over-
stocking. The present population of the 'homelands' is five million; it would be utterly impossible for the 'homelands' to support
the total African population of over twelve million. The South
African government offers the residents in these areas what can
only be termed a spurious self-government.

60% of African schoolchildren are in the 'homelands' and
40% in 'white' areas of the country. Out of a total of 2,397,152
African children in school, 375,728 are in the Xhosa 'homeland'
of the Transkei. There are 1,586 African students in the three
university colleges in the 'homelands'.

The Commission for the Socio-Economic Development of the
Bantu areas within the Union of South Africa – generally known
as the Tomlinson Commission – expressed the judgment in 1954
that the nation – that is, the South African whites – must choose
between complete integration and separate development. In an
exhaustive report, consisting of eighteen volumes, they recom-
mended substantial expenditure on development in the 'homelands'. If this was undertaken they forecast an increase in the
number of Africans who could live in reasonable conditions. In
1951 the population of the homelands had been 3,633,000; if
this development was undertaken, it might increase to 5,312,000
in 1961, to 6,915,000 in 1971, and to 9,000,000 in 1981. But even
so, there would still be Africans in the white areas, 4,622,000 in
1961 and nearly six million in 1981. This was the blue print for
separate development; if it was *not* undertaken, there might be
ten million or perhaps even fifteen million Africans in the urban
areas by the end of the century. The development meant a programme of expenditure estimated at £104,000,000 for the first
ten years and probably twice as much for the second ten years.
This money has not been found. For example, the total expenditure on the homelands for the five years 1956–61 was
£7,900,000. Meanwhile, the population has increased without

the development. South Africa has rejected the alternative of integration but refused to pay for separate development.

The Transkei is the largest of the 286 units which are listed as 'homelands' for non-white people. It is a region of about 60,000 square miles, with between two and three million African inhabitants. It does not have self-government or independence, but it comes nearer to doing so than any other of the 'homelands'. It has forty-five elected MPs and sixty-four MPs representing the chiefs. There are African ministers in the departments of Health, Justice, Agriculture, Education, Finance and Roads and Works, but the senior civil servants and permanent secretaries are all appointed from Pretoria. In addition there are 300 white civil servants administering the area, and the police force is one with that in the Republic. Three-quarters of the total budget is met from the South African government, so that budgets must receive approval. This is also true of decisions made by the Transkei government.

In the early 'fifties the African National Congress (ANC) had about 100,000 supporters. Chief A. J. Luthuli was elected president and declared his commitment to the non-violent methods by which he hoped his people would achieve political freedom.

In 1955 a 'Congress Alliance' brought together the ANC, Asian and Coloured organizations, and the South African Congress of Trades Unions. A Freedom Charter was accepted which sought the participation of all South Africa's people in political and social life.

The response of the government was to charge 156 people with treason. An attempt was made to show that the Congress had advocated violence. All the accused were found not guilty and discharged.

The following years were a time of intermittent violent outbursts, organized and co-ordinated by the two main African political movements, ANC and the Pan African Congress (PAC). The culmination of this period was the tragedy in 1960 at Sharpeville. Here a large but unarmed crowd of men and women were confronted by 300 armed police in armoured cars and were fired on, so far as can be ascertained without provocation. Sixty-nine people were killed, including eight women and ten children; 180 people were wounded. Riots followed in many centres and the government declared a State of Emergency. Mass arrests were made and in April the ANC and PAC were declared unlawful organizations.

The end of freedom to organize political parties drove the African movement underground. Their leaders made preparations to call a three day national strike, and the government prepared partial mobilization. Police and army patrolled locations and on the second day the leaders called off the strike. An underground, militant movement, Spear of the Nation (Mkhonto we Sizwe), was created and published its intentions on 16th December, 1961 in the following terms:

> The time comes in the life of any nation when there remain only two choices: submit or fight. That time has now come to South Africa. We shall not submit and we have no choice but to hit back by all means in our power in defence of our people, our future and our friends . . . the people prefer peaceful methods of change to achieve their aspirations without the suffering and bitterness of civil war. But the people's patience is not endless . . . the government has interpreted the peacefulness of the movement as weakness; the people's non-violent policy has been taken as a green light for government violence . . . without any fear of reprisals. The Mkhonto we Sizwe marks a break with the past. We are striking out along a new road for the liberation of the people.

A number of resistance movements, similar to Spear of the Nation, came into being, including POQO, and a group of white South Africans sympathetic to the African cause called the 'African Resistance Movement'.

A campaign of sabotage followed the banning of the main political parties. When members of the Spear of the Nation were put on trial, they were charged with 200 acts of sabotage. Subsequent legislation and police action, including the massive use of informers, has since restricted violent action by African organizations. Many leaders are now in detention and many are exiles abroad. Only the South African government can give up-to-date and accurate figures for political prisoners; as noted on p. 4, the latest official figure is 1,335. Most are Africans although there are some Coloured. They are usually held on

Robben Island, opposite Cape Town. In addition, there are many thousands of Africans imprisoned for offences under laws such as the Pass Laws and the Immorality Act, which would not be offences in a free country.

The position of the African political leader in South Africa is typified in the person of Nelson Mandela. He is a descendant of the old African ruling class and a qualified lawyer who has bene-fited from the educational process, but he was not accepted into white society. In this he is typical of all educated African leaders. At his trial in 1964 he used the following words:

> We of ANC had always stood for a non-racial democracy, and we shrank from any policy, which might drive the races even further apart than they already were. But the hard facts were that fifty years of non-violence had brought African people nothing but more and more repressive legislation, and fewer rights.
>
> We believed that, as a result of government policy, violence by the African people had become inevitable and that unless a responsible leadership was given to control the feelings of our people there would be an outbreak of terrorism which would cause bitterness between the various races of the country.
>
> We felt that without sabotage there would be no way open to the African people to succeed in their struggle against the principle of white supremacy. All other means of opposing this principle were closed by legislation.

Throughout the last twenty years of Nationalist power the grip of the government on African and Coloured people has steadily tightened. The Group Areas Act, the Native Laws Amendment Act, the Bantu Education Act, and many other Acts, have closed and shuttered the lives of non-whites. We shall see later how much this legislation strips a man of his dignity and divides him from his family or the land.

During the same period the government's power of detention without trial has greatly increased. Powers of censorship are very great. Under the Suppression of Communism Act 1950 anyone held to be a communist can be arrested and tried, or simply detained indefinitely. In 1970, twenty-two African political prisoners who had been acquitted under the Suppression of

Communism Act were held without trial. Students protests were held in Johannesburg and Cape Town, asking for their release, and a number of those involved were arrested.[9]

The definition of a 'communist' in the Act is drafted in very wide terms. It includes these words: ' "Communist" means a person . . . who is deemed by the Governor-General to be a communist on the ground that he is advocating . . . or has at any time advocated . . . the achievement of any of the objects of communism . . .,' which presumably might be held to include an even distribution of wealth. It is common for a person with radical political opinions to be banned from certain areas, including his home, and be restricted to live in a comparatively remote place. Political expression of views distasteful to the government is severely restricted, and the police use very harsh methods.

It is relevant to notice that military expenditure in South Africa in the years 1965–66 of £115,000,000 for internal and external defence, is ten times the average annual expenditure on the whole of African education.

When Dr Verwoerd proclaimed a Republic and South Africa left the Commonwealth, one of the last ties with some of the liberal traditions of Europe was snapped, however ineffective they may have been.

(ii) *South-West Africa*

In the last quarter of the nineteenth century this country was a German colony. The German occupation was marked by several rebellions by the Herero and the German administration suppressed these ruthlessly. The worst was in 1905 when there was a massacre of the Herero and large numbers were forced into exile in Bechuanaland Protectorate while the remnants, numbering about one-third of the original tribe, were uprooted from their lands and made wanderers in the land of their birth.

During the first world war it was occupied by South African forces and came under the military rule of the Allies. In 1920 the League of Nations entrusted the Union of South Africa (then under the sovereignty of the British Crown) with a mandate over

---

[9] A new trial of the political prisoners began on 24th August in Pretoria; the trial of the demonstrators, including three clergymen, on 1st September in Johannesburg.

the territory, to be exercised in the interests of the inhabitants and in accordance with international law. But the spirit of the obligation was not kept. South Africa had apparently hoped to annex the territory outright, and her actions in the 'twenties and 'thirties suggest that this hope never died. The country was thrown open more widely to white settlers and, as in South Africa, was divided into zones, in each of which it was legal for people of one race only to own property or take up permanent residence. Opportunities for African education and advancement were severely limited.

Africans and the League of Nations were shocked when another massacre occurred in 1924 under the personal supervision of the Administrator of Windhoek. A Hottentot tribe, the Bondelswarts, had fought bravely on the South African side during the first world war, but they now rebelled against their new masters. The trouble was sparked off by the imposition of a tax upon the dogs on whose aid the Bondeswarts, who were hunters, were dependent. The Administrator himself led a large force, assisted by aeroplanes, which killed over a hundred men, women and children.

These actions were watched with disquiet by many in the wider community of nations and an attempt was made, through the International Court of Justice, to challenge South Africa's actions, but after years of litigation the suit was dismissed on the ground that the parties had no standing, no decision being recorded on the merits of the case. However, in 1966, the General Assembly of the United Nations passed a resolution depriving South Africa of her mandate and vested the administration of South-West Africa in a Council for South-West Africa (Namibia). It consists of eleven member states whose task is to administer the territory until independence is achieved. But the obvious fact is that this Council is at the moment powerless to act. South Africa administers South-West Africa.

In December 1968 the UN General Assembly asked the Security Council to 'take effective measures' to oust the Republic from South-West Africa. In December the following year the Assembly again asked the Security Council to take 'appropriate measures' to effect the withdrawal of South Africa from the territory. The vote on this occasion was ninety-two to two (South

Africa and Portugal), with ten abstentions, among those abstaining being the United States, Britain and France.

Dr Hilgard Muller, the South African Minister for External Affairs, handed a note to U Thant on 2nd October, 1969, which concluded with the words: 'On no account will we abandon the people of South-West Africa, who for half a century have placed their trust in us to lead them on the path of progress, peace and stability.'

There is now considerable economic development, with growing exports of gold and diamonds, and large-scale expenditure in oil exploration. Some mining is taking place in Native Reserves, but not for the benefit of the Reserves. South-West Africa is a microcosm of Southern Africa's racial policies. The Hereros and Ovambos and other tribal groups are restricted to Reserves, but allowed to come to work as unskilled workers in the homes of the whites, and in the industrial development which is largely for the benefit of the white community.

The recent history of South-West Africa has pointed a very clear moral to thoughtful Africans throughout the continent. It has shown that the following of established legal procedures along constitutional lines does not necessarily lead to justice. The voting at the International Court also made Africans highly sceptical about the power or relevance of international law: they noted that it was judges from white nations who voted in accordance with South Africa's wishes and held that the parties had no standing.[10]

The evidence of resistance in South-West Africa to outside domination is given in the publications of SWAPO (South-West Africa People's Organization), and is also provided in the well-documented trial of thirty-seven South-West Africans at Pretoria in 1968. The speech of the spokesman, Toivo Ja Toivo, is given in Appendix VI. Many of those on trial declared themselves to be members of the church. A second trial of eight resistance fighters took place in 1969. Five were sentenced to imprisonment for life.

(iii) *Rhodesia*

Rhodesia has special links with South Africa that can only be

[10] See Appendix VI, p. 106.

understood in historical terms. It was from the Cape of Good
Hope that Cecil Rhodes planned and carried out the white settlement of Rhodesia which began in 1890. This was to be the first
stage of the fulfilment of his dream of an empire stretching from
the Cape through the heart of Africa to the northern sea board.
The first ten years after the occupation were marked by the violent resistance of the African population. The intrusion of the
white settler and mining prospector into Rhodesia was followed
by wide-ranging police patrols which sometimes led to punitive
action against recalcitrant villagers. In 1893 the Matabele War
crushed Matabele resistance and overthrew Lobengula. In the
following years there was resistance to the collection of hut tax
and the recruiting of labour for the newly opened mines. Dispossession of land and cattle, and grievances caused by harsh and
rudimentary administration, led to the Matabele Rising in March
1896 and the Mashonaland Rising a few months later. Fierce fighting took place throughout Rhodesia for two years before the
rebellions were crushed. Africans in Rhodesia were using the only
force available to them to maintain their identity, as they had
tried to do in their earlier history. During the early years of this
century there were frequent reports of local unrest and renewed
white fears of armed risings. In 1900 and 1902 and again in 1917
there was rebellion in neighbouring Portuguese East Africa, with
some fighting within the north-east Rhodesian border.

> It would be a mistake to isolate the risings from the African
> past of Southern Rhodesia and to treat them as if they were a
> response to a totally new situation . . . There is much reason
> to suppose that the answers found to the problems of how to
> organize more people and how to commit them deeply had
> parallels in the past of Southern Rhodesian Africans. There is
> also reason to suppose that they have a continuing relevance
> to the problems of resistance in the contemporary African
> context.[11]

From the beginning it was quite clear that conquest and occupation were undertaken in the interests of the British South
Africa Company and the white settlers. Thus in 1893 the Duke

[11] T. O. Ranger, *Revolt in Southern Rhodesia*, p. 347.

of Fife predicted at the shareholders' meeting: 'Thousands of our countrymen who are too crowded here will take advantage of the enormous space, the healthful climate and the immense resources which this territory offers to those who will go in and possess the land.' This statement was greeted with enthusiastic applause.

The expectation of large deposits of minerals did not materialize and the company and the settlers turned increasingly towards agriculture, particularly cattle-ranching. Indeed the BSA Company was 'an association formed for the acquisition of gain';[12] the colonists did take 'advantage of the enormous space' and the standard area of a farm was 3,000 acres. Education and social welfare services for the African population were left largely in the hands of missionary bodies.

A visitor to Rhodesia in 1912 (H. Rolin) wrote at the time:

Is the black race overall treated with justice? The rights of the native are protected but is a people well-governed merely because it is not exposed to crimes? Africans are powerless to look after their own interests. The Bantu people of Rhodesia are at the mercy of their European conquerors. The system is conceived totally in the interests of the whites. What dominates all is a pre-occupation with the interests of the whites and the absence of a genuine social policy inspired by the interests of the blacks.[13]

This comment has always been basically true, and still is.

In 1923 Company rule came to an end. The small predominantly white electorate was given a choice: either to join the Union of South Africa as a fifth province or to become, under the Crown, a colony with internal self-government and the control of its own police force and army. The electorate chose the latter. Great Britain never relinquished ultimate constitutional authority, or specific reserve powers of veto in regard to Rhodesian legislation that might discriminate against the Africans. But this power of veto was never exercised. In effect the tiny white population of Rhodesia was free to govern Rhodesia as it wished.

[12] BSA Company Extraordinary General Meeting, January, 1908.
[13] *Les Lois et L'Administration de la Rhodesie*, Paris, Challamel, 1913.

Even though Rhodesia did not constitutionally join South Africa, the colony continued to be greatly influenced by South African discriminatory policies and practices. Legislation modelled on South African racial laws included the following: The Land Apportionment Act, Industrial Conciliation Act, The Immorality Act, The Native Registration Act, African (Regulation and Identification) Act 1958 (amended) and the Urban Areas Act.

When Federation was imposed in 1953 despite strong opposition from the Africans of Nyasaland (now Malawi) and Northern Rhodesia (now Zambia), the seeds of its rapid destruction had already been sown by the conservative attitudes of the dominant partner, Southern Rhodesia. African fears were confirmed when the new Federal Prime Minister, Sir Godfrey Huggins (now Lord Malvern) described the 'partnership' envisaged in the new Constitution as that which exists 'between a horse and his rider'. Under pressure from African nationalists, Southern Rhodesia made some grudging concessions over the policy of social segregation but it was always a case of 'too little too late'. The opposition of Africans in the northern territories gathered pace and the Federal superstructure was brought to an end in the early 'sixties.

The European population was very small until after the second world war. In 1913 there were 25,500; in 1930, 48,000; in 1945, 80,500; in 1950, 125,000 and in 1960, 219,000. For more than forty years most white Rhodesians have felt that their country was much more than a colony; they have never lived under Crown Colony rule and from 1923 have been more than halfway to being a Dominion. There has persisted, however, a small liberal element within the white community which has made occasional moves towards the African majority in attempts at a genuine partnership.

From the end of the last century Africans were encouraged to hope that as they progressed in education and adaptation to the Western manner of life, they would be accepted into the evolving society on the basis of equality. This has been the attitude taken by generations of missionaries, civil servants, educationalists and politicians. It was the old British policy at the Cape, where the law was supposed to be colour-blind. But it had been

defeated in South Africa by the spirit of the Transvaal constitution and in the same way was step by step defeated in Rhodesia.

In November 1965 Mr Ian Smith, the Prime Minister, declared independence illegally. No country recognizes Rhodesia
as an independent state and both the Commonwealth and the
United Nations have invoked economic sanctions against Rhodesia with limited results. Sanctions have affected some farmers
and businesses, and driven the Rhodesian régime to attempt to
diversify its agricultural and industrial output; the economic
development of the country has undoubtedly been retarded.[14]
But the overall political effect so far has been to solidify local
white opinion against the Commonwealth and the United
Nations. Attacks by guerrilla freedom fighters probably have
the same effect on white opinion and do not represent a serious
military threat though they may in time erode white confidence.
They certainly demonstrate the conviction of the fighters that
freedom is worth dying for. Nevertheless Rhodesia survives. She
is buttressed by economic and financial help from her two natural
allies in Southern Africa, South Africa and Portugal; by military
aid also from South Africa and by clandestine assistance economically from some non-African countries.

On 1st March, 1970, Rhodesia declared itself to be a Republic,
and announced an election for the following month on the new
constitution. This was followed by the closing of the consulates
of UN member states in Salisbury, including that of the United
States.

There are no signs within Rhodesia of a significant constitutional opposition to the ruling party, the Rhodesian Front. The
leading African politicians have long since been restricted, or
detained, or have escaped the country in order to serve in exile.

One of the results of the Unilateral Declaration of Independence (UDI) is that the Rhodesian government has lost such in-
ward independence of spirit as it possessed, and is now heavily

[14] The official monthly Digest of Statistics, March 1970, published in
Salisbury, Rhodesia, gives the following figures for all the manufacturing
industries:

1964	100	1967	107.2
1965	108.7	1968	117.8
1966	98.6	1969	133.8

dependent upon its powerful southern neighbour. Almost half of Rhodesia's trade is now with South Africa. That country has no wish to shift her frontier forward to the Zambezi; indeed South Africa is glad to have Rhodesia between herself and the Zambian border. She is no doubt happy to extend her economic and political influence wherever possible, but her main foreign policy in Africa at present is to establish working relations with African independent states; to the attainment of this object the continuing Rhodesian crisis is a hindrance. On the success of her foreign policy depends South Africa's ability to expand as an industrial state with a growing continental market for her products.

During the late 'fifties and early 'sixties attempts were made – particularly through the Central Africa Party – to co-ordinate the political idealism of many Africans with the small but articulate group of white liberals, but events overtook them. Towards the end of the Central African Federation there was a strong move further right by the white settlers. Already the year 1960 witnessed rioting and bloodshed, and the army was called upon to restore order. In November, after the passing of the Vagrancy Act, followed by the Law and Order Maintenance Act, 1,400 people were arrested. African demands for more equal treatment were met by harsh legislation and the use of emergency powers by government.

The people of Rhodesia are not naturally an aggressive people, and do not easily turn to violent actions. But a minority see no alternative but to turn to violent methods. Though the Africans fear and hate violence they are now overwhelmingly sympathetic to the actions of the 'freedom fighters', because they see no hope of justice or political progress through peaceful action. A significant note was sounded in the published pastoral letters of the Catholic Bishops, concerning the proposed constitutional legislation in 1969:

> If they (these laws) should be implemented in a new Constitution, it will be extremely difficult for us effectively to counsel moderation to a people who have been patient for so long under discriminatory laws and are now presented with such extreme provocation.

In the years since the war African protest has taken the form of strikes, such as that in 1948, and later public acts of violence. In 1957 the ANC was formed in Rhodesia to seek for political and social change. Mass meetings and protests followed. A State of Emergency was declared in 1959, the ANC was banned and hundreds of arrests followed.

The African National Congress had been banned before the Rhodesia Front won the 1962 election. After the election, more African political leaders were arrested and detained and some were forced to flee the country; the activities of the banned political parties, Zimbabwe African Peoples Union and Zimbabwe African National Union, have continued in exile. They have organized armed attacks across the Zambezi. In these operations they have been joined by African Freedom Fighters from South Africa and aided by (among others) the Liberation Committee of the Organization for African Unity. Between 1967 and 1970 several invasions and raids have taken place and it is significant that South Africa has found it necessary to come to the aid of Rhodesia with manpower and equipment in an effort to crush the attacks. The leaders of the guerilla fighters realize that theirs will be a painful, long-drawn struggle, but they are nonetheless determined to continue.

(iv) *Angola and Mozambique*

The northern bulwarks of Southern Africa are Angola in the West and Mozambique in the East. The two Portuguese 'provinces', each with more than a thousand miles of coastline, form an effective encirclement of central Africa's industrial heartland. Katanga, Zambia, Malawi and Rhodesia, all depend on the railways running through Portuguese-controlled territory to the ports of Lobito on the Atlantic and Beira and Lourenco Marques on the Indian Ocean.

'We have been in Africa for 400 years, which is rather more than to have arrived yesterday,' said Dr Salazar in 1960. It is true that first contacts were made with North Angola in 1482 and with Mozambique in 1505, but penetration of the interior was insignificant until late in the nineteenth century. During the preceding 300 years, apart from occasional explorers, expeditions to the interior were mainly intended to open a way for the slave trade; no regular administration was established.

In Angola, the Portuguese presence began in 1483. During the following century, some thousands of slaves were exported each year to the sugar estates on the island of Sao Tome, to Lisbon and to the slave markets of the New World. The first official expedition took place in 1520, but until 1575, when the military conquest of Angola began, Portuguese interest remained primarily commercial and missionary. The first period of military subjugation lasted for thirty years and is a record of constant fighting by European forces, supported by locally trained auxiliaries. During this period there was some settlement of Portuguese people as farmers and traders. The completion of the conquest led to an increase in the slave trade to over 10,000 each year.

The seventeenth century is a story of warfare, as the Portuguese extended their supremacy over the areas further from the coast. Until the middle of the nineteenth century Portugal used the military conquest mainly to establish a well-organized slave trade whose value exceeded all other forms of trade. The Portuguese dominion over Angola territory was internationally recognized in the Berlin Treaty of 1885. Thirty years earlier David Livingstone had estimated that there were only a thousand white Portuguese in Angola.

After the Conference of Berlin, 1885, Portugal determined to make her sovereignty effective throughout the two territories. African resistance, however, remained widespread in Mozambique until the campaign of 1897. The Bailundu and Congo campaigns of 1902 and 1913 brought organized fighting in Angola to an end.

In the twentieth century forced labour has been a feature of Angolan life. Young men were sent to the plantations of Sao Tome. In the 'twenties Dr Aggrey of Achimota wrote in detail of the forced labour he witnessed on the roads. This was also disclosed in the Ross report of 1926.

Rebellion broke out again in the north of Angola in 1961. Angolans fought with out-moded fire-arms, with knives and machetes, against the well-armed forces of the government. It is estimated that more than ten Africans were killed to every one government soldier, and that more than 30,000 Africans died. The disturbances spread to southern areas of the country and an uncounted number of Africans have died. Many thousands have been interned in prison camps. The security police organization, PIDE, became the feared instrument of control.

A missionary with many years experience in Angola notes that most of the outstanding Africans who are active in efforts to gain freedom for Angola are committed Christians. This arises from the fact that education has been in the hands of missionaries. He adds:

> African eyes have suddenly opened to see the plunder of their most precious natural resources for the benefit of the white man: their diamonds, iron, forests, fish and – most tragic of all – their topsoil.[15]

The main scenes of military action between Portuguese armies and Africans since 1961 have been in the north and in the central Luanda region. In certain areas the Protestant churches have largely been driven underground.

It is reliably estimated that over 400,000 Angolans have escaped over the border into the Congo since the fighting began in 1961. There are now three main resistance movements, engaged from time to time in violent attacks on the government administration, and seeking to lay the foundations for an independent state in the future. One works from the north, based on the Congo; a second from the east, operating from Zambia, and a third is said to be entirely based in southern Angola. Each movement has a distinct background and orientation; relations between them are now less hostile than they have been in the past.

In Mozambique, Portuguese advances in the sixteenth century were not sustained and before long the Portuguese were confined to the coast and one or two stations on the Zambezi. Effective military conquest did not begin again until the second half of the nineteenth century. Local resistance was overcome by military campaigns, as Portugal sought to establish control over territory confirmed to her in 1885. A succession of military governors pacified one area of the country after another, sup-

---

[15] Gilchrist: *Angola Awake*, p. 80.

pressing the resistance of local chiefs. There was an armed rising in 1917 and it was not until 1920 that armed resistance by the African people was crushed.

One of the immediate results of the period of the conquest was the alienation of large tracts of land, and to this day one of the features of Mozambique is the existence of extensive plantations, usually farmed by settlers or Portuguese companies. Sugar, cotton and sisal are the main plantation crops. This particular form of agricultural development formed the basis for the system of forced labour; this was the reason why all Africans (except the 'assimilated'[16]) were compelled to do six months forced labour each year.

In the first three decades of the twentieth century Portugal made little attempt to develop her colonial resources, save by selling 'contract labour'. From Angola young men were shipped to the cocoa island of Sao Tome into 'modern slavery'. From Mozambique African manpower was virtually sold to South Africa and Rhodesia, the men being sent on a system of indentured labour. In 1910 the Portuguese monarchy gave way to a republic, but after sixteen chaotic years this in turn was overthrown by a military coup which subsequently set up the oldest surviving totalitarian state in Western Europe.

Preoccupied with problems at home, with two world wars and with the Spanish Civil War (1936–39) abroad, the Portuguese government during the next half century paid little attention to the colonies. Economically, socially and politically they stagnated. The 1940 census in Angola revealed that there were only 44,000 Europeans in a population of three and three-quarter million: but after the second world war immigration increased. By 1950 the Europeans numbered 79,000; by 1960 an estimated 200,000 in a total of four and three-quarter million. The growth of the white community in Mozambique was less spectacular,

---

[16] To gain the status of assimilated or 'assimilado' an African had to:
(a) Read, write, speak Portuguese fluently.
(b) Have means to support his family in a Western style.
(c) Be a law-abiding citizen.
(d) Be well educated and westernized.
(e) Make formal application to Portuguese authorities.
An assimilado African had to carry his identification papers, behave as an 'honorary white' and not speak his native language.

but it grew from about 40,000 in 1940 to an estimated 100,000 in 1970.

The purpose of the immigration policy was explicitly stated by Dr Adriano Moreira in 1961:

> We believe it necessary to increase the settlement of *our Africa* by European Portuguese who will make their homes there and find in Africa a true continuation of their country.

The expropriation of African land, the restriction of job opportunities for Africans and the attitude of many new immigrants were important factors in lighting the fuse of revolt in Angola in 1961 and in Mozambique in 1964. They arise from the fact that white immigrants are of the labouring class and thus are in direct competition with Africans, from the fundamental poverty and lack of opportunity of the African peasants (who are 94% of the population) and, finally, from the pattern of disruption caused by migrant labour. The same factors are at work in African hostility to the building of the Cabora Bassa dam in Mozambique. This is destined to be the heart of the biggest hydro-electric complex in Southern Africa and is regarded by Africans as a mighty symbol of white dominance. A massive influx of white settlers is expected to take advantage of the region's economy, benefited by the dam, in which Africans will have little or no share. Already the moving of 24,000 Africans has started, partly because of the vast lake, 150 miles across, that will build up behind the dam and partly to ensure that they will not be able to assist the expected guerilla attacks.

The Liberation Movement in Mozambique has a distinct association with the churches. Most of the leaders have grown out of a Catholic upbringing and education, although some of the leaders have strong roots in the much smaller Protestant churches.

> Mozambique African nationalism was born out of the experience of European colonialism. The source of national unity is the common suffering during the last fifty years spent under effective Portuguese rule. Colonial domination created the basis for a psychological coherence, founded on the experience of discrimination, exploitation, forced labour and other such aspects of colonial rule.

Before the second world war African associations were formed in Mozambique either social or co-operative in purpose, but they were carefully watched by the government. Under cover of this movement, certain political discussions took place. During and after the war African students became more aware of world events as some of them were able to travel for studies to South Africa and elsewhere. Some who attempted to form student organizations were imprisoned and others later escaped overseas and have formed the core of the resistance movement.

In 1947 African urban workers took part in a series of strikes, leading to an abortive uprising in the capital, Lourenco Marques, in the following year. There were many arrests and some deportations to Sao Tome. Forty-nine strikers were killed in later industrial unrest. The last incident in this short period of open protest was in 1963; it was suppressed with some shooting and imprisonment. The most significant event which turned the minds of many Africans towards violence was the incident at Mueda in 1960. In this northern region, the country people staged a large protest meeting which it is alleged was scattered by troops, killing more than 500 of the demonstrators.

The following year witnessed both the rebellion in Angola and the political independence of Mozambique's neighbour, Tanzania. Refugees from Mozambique gathered in Tanzania, and the organized resistance movement came into being.

> Although determined to do everything in our power to try to gain independence by peaceful means, we were already convinced at this stage that a war would be necessary. Armed action appeared to be the only method.[17]

The armed rebellion broke out in northern Mozambique in September 1964.

One further aspect of the situation must be noted. The Portuguese claim to be free from racialism. They say it is open to any African to become 'assimilado' in which case he may have all the privileges of a Portuguese. That of course does not extend so far as permitting him to vote in a free election which may change the government, but this is not permitted in Portugal either. And after four hundred years the number of assimilados only amounts

[17] Eduardo Mondlane, *Freedom for Mozambique.*

to one per cent in Angola, one in a thousand in Mozambique. Theoretically there is equality for black and white in Portuguese territories, but this must be seen against a social and economic system which keeps all the economic and political power in white hands, and restricts African educational opportunities.

This brief survey shows that the history of Southern Africa in comparatively modern times has throughout been a tale of conflict. It is violent history and, in the areas considered, the present political systems are maintained solely by political force, without social cohesion, or general consent. If liberation movements are now violent, this is no new manifestation but the continuation of a long and bitter struggle for liberty and independence.

The armed struggle with which the first invasions were met has been revived for a number of reasons. Under-privileged peasants, migrant labourers, and an increasing number of young educated Africans are seeking for a more just and equal society. Racial discrimination, growing unemployment, a new awareness of world events, and the constant irritation of seeing skilled jobs and higher salaries restricted to the privileged whites – all these have combined to bring the conviction that only a change in the power structure will achieve genuine progress. Behind this lie the memories of conquest and dispossession. But above all, the governments of Southern Africa have made it clear that, in a rapidly changing world, they at any rate do not mean change to take place. They are determined to preserve the present situation as long as they can. This makes them, in the eyes of many Africans, an occupying enemy power, as the Nazis were in France. To such an occupying power, many Africans see resistance as the hard, the courageous, and the moral course and collaboration as the easy line of expediency dictated by fear.

3

Conditions Affecting Thirty Million People

We wrote earlier of 'white domination and black repression'. The following pages illustrate in rather more detail how this works out in the lives of those who are repressed.

(a) The Franchise

In South Africa there was a time – in the Cape Colony and Natal – when non-white men could qualify for registration on the common voter's roll, but even before Union in 1910 such rights had begun to be eroded, first in Natal and later in the Cape, by raising the franchise qualifications. The South Africa Act, which conferred constitutional independence, embodied colour discrimination in statutory form. All non-Europeans, even in the Cape, were debarred from eligibility for membership of parliament by virtue of the colour of their skins. African voters in the Cape, however, though they could not become members, could vote; they remained on a common roll until 1936, when they were placed on a separate roll to elect three white members to the House of Assembly. Even this indirect representation was abolished in 1959. There is thus no representation at all in the Assembly – or indeed in the Senate – of the twelve million Africans who constitute more than two-thirds of the entire population and who outnumber the whites even in the towns.

In the Cape tradition, Coloured and Asian men, like Africans, could have the vote, if they fulfilled certain financial and educational qualifications. But in 1956 the Coloured voters in the Cape were also put on a separate roll and were to be represented by

four white people in the Assembly. Even this indirect representation in national affairs has now ceased. Thus for the non-
whites, political rights have been steadily removed. Coloured
people have now lost all representation in the House of Assembly
and have been given their own Coloured Representative Council. It has forty elected members and twenty appointed by the
government. The Council is restricted in its responsibilities to
local community affairs but the elected majority, without much
hope, press for full parliamentary representation.

In South-West Africa the situation is no different. Although
Africans constitute more than 80% of the population they have
no vote in the affairs of their own country. An 'Ovamboland
Legislative Council' has tribal representation and limited local
responsibilities.

In Angola and Mozambique the franchise is a constitutional
device rather than a human right. For forty years the National
Union has been the one party to enjoy any degree of political
freedom. Other parties have only a clandestine or semi-
clandestine existence, surfacing briefly before elections and returning again to oblivion once the elections are over. This is
equally true of metropolitan Portugal. In 1958 when General
Humberto Delgado contested the presidential election, brief
hopes were aroused that political change might come through
constitutional means: but chicanery at the polls and countless
obstacles placed in his way brought disillusionment to the electorate. Nevertheless the government was sufficiently uneasy to
legislate that in the future the President should be elected by the
National Assembly and not by the popular will. Delgado subsequently went into voluntary exile and was later found murdered
on the Spanish Portuguese Frontier. A similar policy of permission for a temporary opposition party was followed in the 1969
election in Portugal.

Prior to 1961 'assimilated' Africans[1] in Portuguese territories
in Africa did qualify as voters, but since only 1% of Africans in
Angola were 'assimilated' (and less than one in a thousand in
Mozambique), their influence was negligible. The mass of Africans, classified as 'natives', had no access to the franchise. The
difficulties encountered by Africans seeking the status of an

[1] See the requirements for an 'assimilated' on p. 33.

'assimilado' fostered the belief that the system was not designed to effect a gradual transfer of power from the minority to the majority, but was rather a colonialist expedient masking a determination to keep control in European hands. This view was strengthened in 1954 when legislation made assimilate citizenship revocable. However, under the pressure of world opinion, the separate system of law for 'natives' (called the 'indigenato') was suddenly abolished in 1961, and all Africans became citizens. However no real change in status was to emerge for the majority of Africans; a distinction was still drawn between those living in a 'civilized' environment and those still living the traditional tribal life. There is therefore no real access to the franchise.

In Rhodesia the central issue of UDI in 1965 was the refusal of whites to share political power with the majority who outnumber them by almost twenty to one. This was frankly stated in the White Paper introducing the new constitution; the old constitution (said the White Paper) was no longer acceptable to 'the people of Rhodesia' (that is, the whites), because it contains 'a number of objectionable features', the principal ones being that 'it provides for eventual African rule and inevitably the domination of one race by another' and that 'it does not guarantee that government will be retained in responsible hands'.

Under the old constitution, there had been two electoral Rolls, A and B, for which the qualifications were based on education and property – not race. The A roll elected three-quarters of the members of the Assembly and therefore held the power; not one per cent of Africans were in fact qualified to vote on this roll. Still, the opportunity for this proportion to increase was there. The new constitution therefore abolishes the A and B rolls and is frankly based on race; it provides that there shall be fifty European members, elected by non-African voters. There are to be sixteen African members, of whom eight would be returned by a roll of African voters and eight by electoral colleges, consisting of chiefs, headmen and representatives of African councils. Chiefs and headmen are government servants, paid by the the government and liable to dismissal. As the assessment of Africans for income-tax increases, the constitution provides that the number of Africans shall be increased two at a time, until there are twenty-six from electoral colleges and twenty-four elected by the Roll of African voters. There would thus – even in this far distant future – be less than one-quarter of the members directly elected by the overwhelmingly more numerous, but poorer, section of the community. But in fact much of the revenue of Rhodesia is raised by indirect taxation. This at present falls proportionately more heavily on the African population, who do not contribute much in income tax; if economic development led to an increase in the African share of income tax, it would be possible to increase the proportion of direct taxation. As legislation regarding income tax and indirect taxation is controlled by the government, African participation in the government process is thus effectively restricted and controlled.

The Senate will consist of twenty-three senators, ten of whom will be Europeans and ten will be African chiefs, with three senators appointed by the President.

The intention of the new Act is thus made perfectly clear. 'The domination of one race by another' is objectionable only if the present situation is reversed; the constitution aims at maintaining present domination indefinitely.

(b) Residence and Work

Residence In South Africa the residential areas are strictly zoned, in accordance with apartheid policies, so that a non-white needs special permission to live anywhere outside restricted geographical areas. An African cannot visit a town or city and remain there for more than seventy-two hours without a special pass; not even if he was born there and is now returning after an absence of some years; not even if he had worked for the same employer there for eight or nine years and now wishes to return.

A single man working in the town, who wishes to marry a woman from the rural areas, cannot do so and remain in the town with his wife. He has to marry a woman already in that town or in another urban area. Even when marriages are made in the towns they are fraught with difficulties. Consider an actual case. An African girl had worked as a housemaid in a white home in Cape Town. She had lived only nine years in Cape Town, not ten, and was therefore not entitled to be regarded as a resident. When she married, she was 'endorsed out': this means that she was ordered to leave, the object being to prevent the growth of an urban population. She was forcibly put on the train to Kimberley with which her only link was that, many years before, she had nursed a sick uncle there who had long since died. She had no relations in Kimberley, no home to go to, no job. Her marriage one month old, she was subject to indefinite separation from her husband, who would lose his job and his residential qualification of ten years if he left Cape Town to rejoin his wife, and who in that case might easily find himself endorsed out of Kimberley.

When a man gets work in town it is as a migrant labourer, and his permission to remain is only valid while he is under contract to a particular employer for a specified time. He cannot bring his wife from the rural areas with him. As an African clergyman stated in 1964: 'Stringent regulations now compel African men to live for 353 days of the year away from their wives.'

In 1968 there were 1,664,000 single Africans from the 'homelands' working in white areas, and in that year 61,658 unemployed Africans were sent back to the 'homelands', already overcrowded. They arrive every week, sometimes with no surviving friends or relations and nowhere to go.

The cause of these indignities lies in the Group Areas Act, the Bantu Laws Amendment Act and similar legislation. The Group Areas Act permits property ownership and residential rights only in areas defined on rigidly racial lines. Under this act a few whites and hundreds of thousands of non-whites are being required to move. It is estimated that over a million people will be forced to move home in the next few years. Often the new areas set aside are far from town and lack basic facilities. The removal scheme at Limehill, Natal, became notorious because of the way in which Africans were forcibly removed to an area without proper sanitary or medical facilities. Many of the people being moved are Coloured or Asians. For example, all the Indians in [Johannesburg and] Durban will eventually have to go to Lenasia and Chatsworth, [respectively;] ~~about twenty miles south-west of the city~~; all the coloured people of Cape Town and the adjoining municipalities are being moved to new housing schemes on the Cape Flats, a far less desirable area than the city area where they once lived which is now reserved for whites. The consequence for Indian shopkeepers and Coloured property owners can be imagined. This re-arrangement of population on racial lines is taking place in hundreds of urban communities.

This might suggest that residential restriction only operates in the urban areas. This is far from the truth. An African has no legal right to live in the vast 'European' rural areas. His presence there is controlled by an Act of 1936, as amended in 1964. Even within the 'homelands' or Bantustans, the African cannot live exactly where he wishes. Since 1957 no incoming African may take up residence in a particular place except under stringent conditions. Black is separated from black in terms of ethnic sub-groupings. Thus apartheid splinters the black community as well as dividing white from black.

At the time of the census in South Africa in April 1970, it was estimated that there were over 10,000 Africans living illegally in the big African township of Soweto, Johannesburg. They were hidden within the population of over 600,000 African workers, having earlier been sent from the municipal areas to the 'homelands', from which they had surreptitiously returned.

In reply to questions in the Assembly on 7th February, 1969[2] the Minister of Community Development said that, as a result of the proclamation of group areas, up to 30th September, 1968, the following families became disqualified to remain in their homes:

656 White families
58,999 Coloured families
784 Chinese families
35,172 Indian families

Those who have been 'resettled' in group areas by that date were:

497 White families
23,587 Coloured families
17,723 Indian families

According to information given to Parliamentarians who visited resettlement schemes in 1969, 25,156 African families have been moved[3] from areas that were allocated to Indian, Coloured, or

[2] Hansard 1 cols. 303,312.
[3] *Rand Daily Mail*, 27th August, 1969.

White people. It is hardly necessary to emphasize what these compulsory moves mean in human terms.

The South African Institute of Race Relations has summed up the position clearly: 'Africans now require permission to live anywhere at all'. This is almost the final indignity for African people. The land has traditionally been very closely associated with the meaning of life itself and the psychic security of many Africans is seriously disturbed and undermined by its withdrawal.

To non-white South Africans it seems that most white South Africans think that they can be beckoned like children or slaves to do the necessary tasks – the cities are crowded with Africans for this purpose – and then shooed back to the reserves. There they can play at government provided they keep quiet. While they are in the cities they must move obediently as voteless, faceless individuals without rights or roots. They are not wanted there. They are just needed.

Work in Towns   From the early days of South Africa, Africans have been required to carry 'passes'. This was always an indignity, but in 1952 the pass-system was transformed into a more precise and effective weapon of control, often opening the way to victimization. By an Act passed in that year it became compulsory for every African to possess and carry his reference book on pain of arrest. In it are included his photograph and finger prints and details of permission to work, to travel, and almost to exist. African life is in effect controlled by the contents of these books and by the officials of the labour bureaux who make their entries in them. Any African can, at any time and without reason given, be stopped by the police and required to show his reference book. In 1967/8, the number of people convicted on pass and similar offences was 937,098. The daily average of prosecutions for pass offences alone is now 2,000. To be charged with a pass offence almost always means arrest and detention for at least one night in the cells. The power which this puts in the hands of the police is obvious.

We have already noted the difficulty that the African meets in getting work in the urban areas. However there is a further hazard which blocks his way in town and country.

Job Reservation   Reservation in favour of the whites (and sometimes Coloured people) has been traditional in South Africa for
many years. At one time there were many jobs for which no
Africans had the training and therefore the skill; they were not
unnaturally able to obtain only unskilled jobs and even for these
they received much lower wages than a white man. But what
began as a matter of skill became a legally enforced distinction
and Africans were effectively prevented from getting the training that would have given them the skills needed for higher
wages. The law of 1911 reserving certain jobs in the gold mines
for whites merely recognized and enforced long-standing practice. But the policy was carried much further after the first world
war, when white unemployment was wide-spread. It was known
as the 'civilized labour' policy; and there has been a steady extension of the jobs to which it applies.

The four major Acts which give effect to the colour bar and
the civilized labour policy are the Mines and Works Act of 1911,
amended in 1926 to reinforce the colour bar in the mines; the
Apprenticeship Act of 1922; the Industrial Conciliation Act of
1924; and the Wage Act of 1925. These have since been amended
several times. Between them, they prevent Africans, and to a
lesser extent other non-whites, from entering skilled trades in
such industries as building, engineering and printing. Since 1956
all Africans have been excluded from Trade Unions which may
register under the Industrial Conciliation Act and in the same
year amendment to the Act forbade the formation of any new
Trade Unions that were racially mixed; existing mixed unions
had to form separate racial branches. Africans are also forbidden
to strike. The success of the policy is shown by the Report of the
Department of Labour in 1956. This stated that in a group of
industries investigated by the Wage Board, of 117,000 workers
classed as skilled, 83% were white and only 6% were African,
though the Africans were four times as numerous in the population. As to wages, in 1886 an African labourer in the diamond
mines collected between 7s 6d and 8s 6d per week: a European,
£4 to £8 per week. By the end of the nineteenth century, general
wage levels were something like £1 a day for the white mines
supervisor or artisan and something under £1 a week for the

African labourer. This proportion has not been substantially changed. The 1968 survey of Race Relations in South Africa declares:

> The job reservation determinations are designed to protect White workers from non-white competition. A few of them also protect Coloured and Asians from African competition. In general, Coloured and Asian advancement (i.e. to more skilled jobs) is possible as long as the minimum rate for the job is paid. A certain measure of African advancement in operative jobs is allowed for too (except in mining), but the closed shop principle may be applied in the skilled grades of work, thus excluding Africans because *they cannot be members of registered trade unions.*[4]

There is in South Africa an acute shortage of white workers and a surplus of non-white workers. Yet government policy is to extend the restriction on non-whites occupying skilled and semi-skilled places in urban areas. In 1970 the range of restriction was extended to include shop-assistants, telephonists, clerks, typists and others. This is defended on the ground that Africans must seek skilled employment in the areas specially reserved for them, where of course the jobs do not exist.

It will be seen from this brief review that Africans in South Africa are denied freedom of residence and of work to such an extent that both justice and human dignity are deeply affronted. How can a man and his wife and family grow together and advance towards fulfilment in such conditions?

In South-West Africa the situation is similar; the movement of Africans is restricted and the system of apartheid is pursued with the same vigour. For example, part of the Herero tribe is now being forced to leave its traditional land and move to a less desirable area near the Botswana border.

Windhoek, the capital, with a population of about 70,000 is a white city. The Africans (22,000) live at Katutura several miles outside the city, and the Coloured (10,000) live at Khomasdal. Segregation is strictly enforced in the city, with separate entrances at banks and post-offices, and separate means of public

[4] See *A Survey of Race Relations in South Africa*, 1969, p. 114.

transport. Africans cannot belong to registered Trade Unions and are forbidden to strike. Because of their low economic position and lack of training facilities most Africans are effectively hindered from joining most occupations and professions.

In Angola and Mozambique a rigid pass system has been in operation for many years. It was used in such a way that any African who was not classed as assimilado – and this as we have seen was ninety-nine per cent of the African population – was in practice liable to six months labour on the roads unless he had been in regular employment during the previous year. Night raids on villages have been a commonplace for generations, men being taken off for periods of 'contract' labour, which could be renewed if substitutes from their villages were not forthcoming. In law craftsmen and planters with a certain turnover were exempt, but in practice the sanctions of law were often evaded and such exemptions were often disallowed. After 1945 the application of this system was intensified as the post-war boom increased the demand for labour. In Angola the needs of the plantations in the north, the fisheries in the south, the diamond mines in the interior and of the government everywhere, led to increasingly close attention being paid to the movement of men. As a result large numbers emigrated to the Congo and other neighbouring countries. Women and children also were recruited for road work, the sorting of coffee and other tasks. When Portugal was accepted into the United Nations (1955) contracts were theoretically introduced in place of the old system of forced labour, but the legislation on the statute book was generally ignored and the old system continued.

In Mozambique, Conventions with South Africa (1926) and with Rhodesia (1934) provide for the sending of approximately 160,000 workers annually to those countries. In return a large proportion of South African and Rhodesian exports are channelled through the ports of Lourenço Marques and Beira.

Freedom of association in the Portuguese territories is severely limited for both white and black, irrespective of colour. Trade unions are controlled by the government and have no effective bargaining power.

In Rhodesia when an African comes to work in the towns he finds that he is confined to specific African townships which may be many miles from his work. He has no freehold rights. He cannot move without a certificate of registration. Job reservation is achieved in favour of the whites partly by the control of secondary education and partly, as in South Africa, by the Trade Union and conciliation procedure. The average annual earnings of a white man are more than ten times that of an African. In practice there is an almost complete colour bar to the professions. The present regime, the Rhodesian Front, favours an even more complete segregation of the races.

The Land Tenure Act (1970) sets aside roughly 44,000,000 acres for the 220,000 whites and 44,000,000 acres for the 4,300,000 Africans, excluding forest and national reserve. The re-arrangement which this legislation will cause, if it is put into effect, will mean the transfer of many communities from traditional areas, as under the Group Areas Act of South Africa. One of the remarkable features of the proposals is the arbitrary power of the President, and the Minister, in reaching decisions regarding land allocation. This new land legislation has been strongly opposed by church leaders in Rhodesia, not only because of the challenge to long-standing missions, but also because of the racial implications.

(c) Severely limited educational opportunities

In all five territories the natural wish of the people is for more education for their children. Secondary education is thought to be a key to wider opportunity and the withholding of it is viewed with suspicion and anger.

In South Africa education for white children is compulsory and free up to the age of sixteen and a third of the white children of school-going age are in secondary schools. But the education of non-white children is on a different basis, dictated by the Bantu Education Act of 1953, the Coloured Persons' Education Act of 1963 and the Indians' Education Act of 1965. This fulfils Dr Verwoerd's injunction, 'Education must train and teach people in accordance with their opportunities in life according to the sphere in which they live. . .'.[5] Apartheid in education has resulted in the following disparities: Expenditure on the education of each racial group: Africans 9%, Europeans 77%,

[5] House of Assembly, 17th September, 1953.

Coloureds 10% and Indians 4%[6] of total government expenditure on education. The Matriculation passes reflect the apartheid caste structure: Africans 0·13%, Whites 15·3%, Coloureds
0·54% and Indians 1·37%[7] of admissions to school for that racial
group. It should also be noted that the percentage of matriculation passes in Bantu education schools has rapidly declined from
47·3% of candidates in 1953 to 17·9 in 1960.[8] We are aware that
much has been made of the vast increase in numbers enrolled in
the primary school since the start of Bantu education, but this
has been done by reducing the teaching time and doubling the
number of pupils per teacher in the sub-standards. Between
1953 and 1963 the number of pupils increased by 91%, but the
number of teachers increased by only about one-third and the
amount of money available increased by only 36%.[9]

If as a result of great effort and good fortune African parents
manage to have their son or daughter go to a university it will be
to a racially and tribally segregated college. This is the result of
the Extension of University Education Act of 1959. None of
these tribal colleges has an Engineering Department, and scien-
tific and technological facilities are very poor. Fort Hare, which
had reached high academic standards, was effectively broken up
by being limited to one tribal group.

In the non-white colleges, there is very little freedom of speech
and association. Members of staff are civil servants and liable to
dismissal for political reasons. The training, too, is designed for
apartheid purposes. Lawyers and social workers are being trained
to serve non-white clients. African dentists will be permitted to
draw non-white teeth. African doctors will lawfully extract non-
white appendixes. There is, too, a wide discrepancy between the
remuneration for the qualified African and the European.

In South-West Africa education is also segregated; there are
even poorer opportunities for Africans than in South Africa.
There are no secondary schools with fifth and sixth forms for
Africans. Conditions for coloured children are little better.

---

[6] South African Institute of Race Relations Survey 1967.
[7] South African Statistical Year Book for 1964.
[8] Minister of Bantu Education, House of Assembly, 14th February, 1961.
[9] 'A Decade of Bantu Education' by Muriel Horrell.

There is no African doctor from the area in the whole territory.

In Angola and Mozambique the education of 'natives' was traditionally entrusted to Christian missions. Some subsidies were available to Catholic missions but none to Protestant. The state accepted direct responsibility only for the schooling of Europeans and 'assimilados'. In Angola in 1956 there were approximately 50,000 pupils in mission schools and 15,000 in government and private schools. Less than 4,000 children were in secondary and technical education. The government grant to education in that year was one-tenth of a penny per head of the population: one per cent of the population attended school: the illiteracy rate was given as ninety-nine per cent.

In Mozambique the missionary presence has been much smaller, subsidies for education purposes meagre, and the illiteracy rate more than ninety-nine per cent.

After the outbreak of revolt in Angola (1961) and Mozambique (1964) the government took a new interest in the education of Africans. It was alleged that mission education had been inefficient, that it had contributed to the disaffection leading to rebellion and that it was too literary. John Gunther quotes a Mozambique Education Ministry official:

Frankly we do not want *many* educated natives, until they have an appropriate social background. They have no place to go. They become dissatisfied. What we want here is a stable society, a stable state. So we move very, very slowly.[10]

These views affected the methods used. Troops not in the fighting line were used to organize schools. The building of village schools in local materials, which had been pioneered by missions in spite of government opposition, was now encouraged by those who had opposed them. At the same time, obstacles were placed in the way of mission schools. As in South Africa education is becoming much more subject to state control.

The increase in the European population has meant a demand

[10] *Inside Africa*, John Gunther, p. 581.

for more secondary schools and the beginning of a university, but opportunities for Africans are restricted by social and economic factors which can only be altered by government intervention. While theoretically children of all races have an equal opportunity, white privilege is firmly entrenched.

In Rhodesia also education follows the pattern we have come to expect. Every white child is given the opportunity of primary and secondary schooling. Only one African child in twenty has the opportunity of secondary education. Two per cent of the government's annual budget is spent on African education and 10% on European education. This apparent equality conceals a gross injustice at the root of the educational system in Rhodesia because there are many times more African children than European.

The restriction on African higher education can be seen in the facilities for sixth form work. The total annual intake for African children in the sixth forms is 180 places. Some of these places are in schools which have been developed by the churches, the churches themselves providing the capital funds. It is extremely difficult for the churches to obtain permission to double-stream at the 'A' level, or to open schools providing sixth-form work. There is a supplementary scheme of vocational secondary training (two years) for some African children which educationalists view with grave misgivings.

At one time some encouragement was found in the fact that the University College at Salisbury was founded as a multi-racial institution and began in affiliation with London University. The University College today is working under difficulties, and is viewed with some distrust both by the government and the African majority. The fact remains that here at least Africans and Europeans are being trained together. There are 464 European students and 403 African and other races. Racial tensions are likely to increase when the University College becomes independent of London and Birmingham, as will shortly be the case.

Another crucial area of failure in African education in Rhodesia is that very few African children are being trained for technical skills or are allowed into the apprenticeship system. Africans are not being prepared for skilled occupations in commerce and industry.

(d) Police victimization

It is hard for a citizen of the United Kingdom to conjure up the image of a policeman as he is known to the non-whites in these territories. The policeman is not seen as a friendly helper of young and old, but as the agent of an oppressive and indeed hostile government.

In South Africa the police are a semi-military organization with wide powers of arrest, without warrant, leading frequently to detention without trial. Every white constable carries a gun; African constables all carry batons. No African policeman of any rank may arrest a white person. No non-white policeman may guard a white man in his cell. About half the police force is non-white and most of those are African. That such a large number of Africans are willing to serve as police constables may seem surprising but the police are comparatively well-paid, secure and pensionable, and jobs are scarce. Once in the police, there is obvious danger in leaving before a man's time is expired; depending on circumstances, he may be a target of resentment to his former colleagues or to the general public, or even to both. On the other hand, to be in the police gives power and many opportunities for illegal gratification. On the pretext of looking for beer brewed against the law, or on other legalized pretexts, the police have unlimited rights of access to African homes; they may stop any African in the street and demand his registration book.

But this is not all. There are strong allegations that torture is used both by the uniformed branch and by the security force. It is widely believed that beatings of the accused have been supplemented by electric shock torture. The 90-day law of 1963, the 180-day law and the Terrorist Act of 1967, give the security police opportunities to pursue their enquiries without any control by court or public opinion. Statue torture,[11] sleep deprivation and electric shock are alleged to be the main weapons used against victims detained without trial and in solitary confinement up to 180 days: indeed since 1967 for an indefinitely long period. The allegations were fully discussed in the Gander/Pogrund Trial in 1969, and are supported by the evidence of many

[11] In this torture the victim is forced to stand for hours and even days on one spot without moving.

individuals.[12] The people said to have been involved in such treatment have been African, Coloureds, Asians and Whites, but by the nature of the South African situation, Africans are the most frequent victims of police injustice and brutality.

In South-West Africa police powers are similar. Under an Act of 1922 an African without his pass in an area at a distance from his work or residence may be arrested without warrant. Banning orders may be issued in South-West Africa as well as in South Africa under the Suppression of Communism Act 1950. There is indeed no apparent difference between suffering under the police in South Africa and South West Africa. Over forty nationalist leaders from South-West Africa are detained in South Africa.

In Angola and Mozambique harsh treatment by the civil police was all too common before the introduction of the secret police (PIDE) in the middle 'fifties. Their arrival led to a more relentless and more brutal network being set up, with informers and *agents provocateurs*. It is widely alleged that not only detention without trial but beatings, statue torture and electrical shock treatment are being used.

The coming of PIDE was part of the government response to the growth of African nationalist movements. In Angola the Peoples' Movement for the Liberation of Angola was formed in 1956 as a result of the coming together of a number of smaller groups two years earlier; in 1954 the Union of the Populations of Angola had been formed in Leopoldville amongst expatriate Angolans. Other parties followed, of which the most important was PDA (or ALIAZO as it was first called), and later the National Movement for Total Independence of Angola. These parties made representations to the Portuguese government and later to the United Nations. For two years, from March 1959 to February 1961, the only response from the government was to intensify police action, to imprison, to torture, to kill. So in March 1961 the Angolans countered violence with violence.

In Mozambique the same process has been followed. The arrogance of dictatorship permits of no real debate. Public criticism, with the notable exception of the Bishop of Beira, was virtually unknown. Political parties operated underground. The

[12] For evidence, see A. Sachs, *The Violence of Apartheid*, pp. 45–53.

police became ruthless. The deterioration ended in the outbreak of guerilla war in 1964.

In Rhodesia the story is not very different. At one time, the rural population had some confidence in the impartiality of the police, but in the towns today this has broken down entirely. There is perhaps a more natural relationship between the African constable and the African people, but Rhodesia has long been governed by Emergency Regulations which have given the police wide powers of arrest. There have been many cases showing that these wide powers have brutalized those who exercise them. Even before UDI (November, 1965) 1,791 Africans and two coloured persons were detained between January 1964 and August 1965, either in prisons or in camps. Many Africans, some coloured people, and a few whites have also been restricted without trial; the latest official figures at the time of writing are 211 in restriction and 142 in detention, all without trial.

The Reaction to these Indignities

Let us look at the overall effect of these many impositions and indignities suffered in varying degrees of intensity by thirty million people. They are not separate sufferings but an accumulation of pain and frustration felt in the societies of five similar states. Each government perhaps imagines that the strong tie that binds together their separate countries is the policy of white supremacy; but there are other common ties: the anguish, and the persistent hope of the people who are being oppressed. This deep resistance cannot finally be denied and must eventually challenge oppression. In the whole of Southern Africa there is a deep longing for greater freedom and for human dignity. In each of the territories some people endure long periods of imprisonment, as a direct result of their struggle for liberation; the majority endure humiliating conditions with few grounds for hope.

It may well be asked, how is it that the African people have been patient for so long? We have tried to show that there was long resistance to the white invasion. But once it was an accomplished fact, there was often a measure of acquiescence. This was due in part to the courtesy which many Africans achieve in testing circumstances. Furthermore, there was a period when the

black inhabitants of Southern Africa were profoundly awed by
the mastery of the white man in many fields as well as by the
gun in his hand. There was real admiration of many typically
white qualities, sometimes even genuine personal affection.
Often there was dissimulation in the face of superior force; sometimes, the same African heart alternated between these moods.
But during the twentieth century, and in some places before its
beginning, a new concept has been born: that one day their
country would once more become their own. The 1939–45 war
greatly accelerated the understanding of this concept and deep-
ened the resolve to make it true.

In all five territories the 'fifties were a most significant decade.
Political parties gathered or renewed their strength. In South
Africa there came into being the African National Congress; in
South-West Africa, the Ovamboland Peoples Organization; in
Angola MPLA, PDA and other parties; in Mozambique, Frelimo; in Rhodesia the African National Congress. The 'fifties
and 'sixties also saw a time of increasing suppression by the
authorities of all forms of political resistance. Resistance to the
status quo in these territories has included attempted constitutional reform through the activity of political parties, protests
by both men and women against pass laws or similar restrictions,
and the use of boycotts and strikes. There have been protests
and revolts, not only in the towns but in the rural areas. One of
the most moving and tragic examples of non-violent protest was
that at Sharpeville, to which we have already referred.[13] This
was one of the last of a long series of attempts at non-violent demonstrations. It seems that the 21st March, 1960 – the date of
Sharpeville – marked a turning point for many. Albert Luthuli
was to be followed by more aggressive leaders of resistance
like Nelson Mandela and Robert Sobukwe. After the African
National Congress and the Pan African Congress were banned
in 1960, the movement has continued underground.

In South-West Africa more recently there has been a similar
shift from constitutional and non-violent means of reform to a
more violent approach. In Angola and Mozambique, too, constitutional methods of redress have been attempted prior to 1960
(Angola) and 1963 (Mozambique). A similar trend has been seen

[13] See page 19.

in Rhodesia. Vigorous political activity in the 'fifties was followed by the banning of parties in the 'sixties.

There has been a fresh factor in the situation since the early 'sixties. World opinion has become alive to the extent of the problem in a new way. The independent nations of Africa, the Commonwealth organization, and the United Nations, have all reacted more positively to the Southern Africa situation. The international student community has become involved more profoundly in the issues, and world Christian opinion has been more vocal. This has brought some small encouragement to millions caught in the prisons of their own lands. To many Africans the most heartening sign has been the increasing activity of the Organization for African Unity (OAU) and its Liberation Committee. It was the secretary of the OAU who declared that 'apartheid is the most abominable symbol of the worst humiliations which for centuries have been imposed upon Africans'.

The Liberation Committee represents nine African countries and has its headquarters in Dar-es-Salaam. It supervises and supports the military activity of liberation movements in Southern Africa. At the time of writing the governments of South Africa, the Portuguese territories and Rhodesia are infinitely stronger militarily than any regular African forces that could be marshalled against them. The liberation movements face immense strategic, tactical, economic and administrative problems and are not yet a formidable military presence.

The guerilla movement, however, is not insignificant. In the whole area under consideration the movements engaged in opposition to the established governments, in organization of small occupied areas and in military activities, are as follows:

South Africa	African National Congress	ANC
	Pan African Congress	PAC
S.W. Africa	South-West Africa People's Organization	SWAPO
Rhodesia	Zimbabwe African Peoples' Union	ZAPU
	Zimbabwe African National Union	ZANU

Mozambique	The Mozambique Liberation Front	FRELIMO
Angola	The Peoples Movement for the Liberation of Angola	MPLA
	National Movement for Total Independence of Angola	UNITA
	Revolutionary Government of Angola in Exile	GRAE

All these movements have offices in European capitals and elsewhere, and some have headquarters in Africa. The OAU Liberation Committee grants recognition to the leading movements, and is a means for providing them with material support. Financial support is also received from some Western and European countries, as well as from Russia and China. The OAU Humanitarian Institute in Dar-es-Salaam channels funds for medical aid to the liberation movements.

In January 1969 a conference of some liberation movements was held at Khartoum in the Sudan. Many of the leaders of these movements are well-known to both political and church leaders in Africa and the Western world. Naturally, they do not seek publicity, and are seldom in the news.

Some outside governments have provided training programmes for freedom fighters, and many hundreds of Africans have been sent to training centres in African, Asian and European countries. Some of the training courses in guerilla fighting have been of four or five years' duration, and included ambitious and advanced techniques.

Recruits for the movement come chiefly from refugees and the large number of unemployed in every African country. The number of refugees in Africa, mainly for political and tribal reasons, has now reached the figure of 1,500,000. An independent assessment of the total number of young Africans at organized training centres for guerilla fighters is given as 8,000. No African governments have sent service contingents to join liberation movement campaigns.

Some of the activity of the movement is directed against industrial installations which serve the established regimes, and other activities cause the authorities to maintain garrisons. The Benguela Railway in Angola and the development at Cabora Bassa in Mozambique are examples of objectives which are sometimes mentioned as targets.

In the Portuguese territories the guerilla fighters are causing Portugal to maintain 150,000 troops in Africa and to devote 40% of her budget to military expenditure. Yet it is there that guerilla leaders see the clearest prospects of success. It would be a mistake, however, to imagine that the leaders expect success within a few years; they are prepared for a long struggle which may last for decades. They see the present policies of Rhodesia and South Africa, with the inevitable population growth, as contributing to the strengthening of revolutionary forces.

The roles of Russia and China in this movement are real. Arms, finance and training are being provided by both, though there is some disagreement between observers as to the scale. Revolutionary groups are always in competition for resources and are apt to disagree on methods and tactics; the conflict between Russia and China has added further grounds for division, since some groups are loyal to one and some to the other. However, the revolutionary movement as a whole is likely to gather momentum, and the involvement of Russia and China is likely to become greater rather than less, as they compete for leadership.

In South-West Africa the South-West African People's Organization (SWAPO) is operating. Thirty-seven of its leaders and associates were taken out of their own country in 1967 and tried in Pretoria. Twenty-nine prisoners were sentenced, nine of them for life. Some of these were in the guerilla movement which had been operating in 1966 and 1967.

In Mozambique there has been a strong internal revolutionary movement, led from 1962 until his recent death by Dr E. Mondlane. The revolution itself began in 1964 in the Cabo Delgadi and the Niassa provinces. The Mozambique guerilla movement (Frelimo) has been until recently in control of some of the rural areas, and has made sporadic attacks on the central provinces of Tete and Zambesi: and in the district where the Cabora Bassa Dam is to be built. In Angola the revolt began in 1961. It has been severely repressed by fighting, intimidation and imprisonment and it is estimated that more than 400,000 Africans have fled the country. Some of the liberation movements work from outside the country and some from within, with different international support.

These separate activities have met with strong resistance from the South African, Portuguese and Rhodesian forces. In Rhodesia, South African para-military police units have joined the Rhodesian forces and police. It is generally believed that the governments have co-ordinated their military activity in response to the challenge of the violent, revolutionary movements.

In assessing this whole movement, it is important to recognize how an uncritical use of terms may determine attitudes. 'Terrorists' is an emotive term used by opponents of the guerillas. Is it justified? It ought surely to describe those who use terror to gain or maintain power. This is not accurately descriptive of the liberation movements in Portuguese territories or in Rhodesia; it might become an accurate description if they were more successful. It does, on the other hand, describe accurately the governments in these countries, which are far more successful in arousing terror and in maintaining power. We believe, therefore, that it should not be used. The majority describe themselves as 'liberation movements'. If their aim is an enlargement of human freedom, they will be judged by the degree of their achievement. 'Freedom Fighters' is also descriptive of an aspiration. 'Guerilla Fighters', 'Insurgents', or 'Armed Revolutionaries' are terms which could perhaps most accurately be used, without being pejorative.

It is clear that the growth of violent movements in Southern Africa in the 'sixties offers no prospect of peace in the immediate future. There is no immediate hope of success. It is undeniable, further, that it will lead to an increase in bitterness between the races, and be destructive of some of the limited understanding which exists between groups of black and white. This trend is already very noticeable. Africans and Europeans within some institutions such as universities or the churches, who used to be open and understanding to one another, are so no longer. The drift apart has developed as, on the one hand, the African has seen the formidable strength and inflexible nature of entrenched white privilege and, on the other, the European sees every day more clearly that the position of dominance and exploitation can only be maintained by absolute power.

It is the unquestioned power and implacable nature of the economic and political white structures which partly determines the basic attitude of the African. Disillusionment has replaced hope; non-violent protest has resulted in intimidation and brutality, and now there only remains to him endurance, patience and struggle.

No sensible person can doubt that in all five territories there are many Africans who are hardly affected by political movements and who are concerned mainly with the material problems of their lives. There are others who have deliberately chosen a quiet life rather than trouble with police, others who sincerely believe it is an overriding Christian duty to suffer in silence. But in every occupied or colonial country, there have been these passive elements. Again and again their ultimate sympathies have been shown to lie with the Resistance, or whatever is the equivalent, rather than with the forces of occupation. There is evidence – which obviously cannot be made public – that this is so in Southern Africa also.

We shall consider in chapter 5 the problem of the Christian attitude to this violent, and, in the short term, hopeless struggle, which aims nonetheless, in the long term, at justice and freedom.

4

What of the Future?

(i) *An Assessment of what is probable in Secular Terms*

What developments are likely for the future? Let us first look at the likelihood in purely secular terms. It is easier to be negative than positive. Southern Africa may be regarded as a fortress of white supremacy, South Africa being the inner keep while the outer bastions are Rhodesia, Angola, Mozambique and the former High Commission territories. There are those who believe that the entire fortress will fall because of disagreement within the garrison of the inner keep; there are those who think that the only chance of success is to storm one by one the outer bastions. Hopes of a split within the National Party recur periodically; every few years some visitor to South Africa comes back with news of a split which will rend the party from top to bottom. But the result so far has always been the same; the party closes in on itself before the crack becomes wide enough to weaken it. If the United Party came into power – and even after the 1970 election this does not appear likely in the foreseeable future – there would still be no prospect of any solution; it is inconceivable that any African leader with wide support could accept United Party policy. One must conclude that the white parties in South Africa present a solid front and will not by their own disagreements fall apart. This is because they have so much to lose; white people in South Africa enjoy a standard of living which they could not possibly hope to maintain if their privileged position came to an end, as it would be bound to do under majority rule.

If the centre is unlikely to crack, can the bastions be stormed? The whites in Rhodesia are also divided in their emphasis but they too have so far shown a remarkable power of solidifying in the presence of outside threats. The incursions of guerillas will erode white confidence and security and will strain the financial and military resources of Rhodesia, but guerillas cannot hope for military success in the open plains of the greater part of the plateau country. By keeping the armed forces on the alert and increasing the level of taxation they may speed up the emigration of some white Rhodesians but in present circumstances they seem unlikely to achieve military victory. They will, however, keep the anger of their people before the world; some would argue that the assertion of their passionate belief has an absolute value of its own.

It might conceivably be argued that Portugal may come to see the situation as France and Britain have done; both these countries decided for a variety of reasons that it was against their interest to maintain by military force their rule in countries which wished for independence; it seemed possible that they would stand in a better relationship of every kind and also have a better prospect of maintaining trade if they gave up political rule. Portugal is too small, and the structure of her export system too limited, to make such a calculation. So long as the present Portuguese regime lasts, any voluntary withdrawal is improbable.

It is believed by some that economic development will inevitably, if gradually, break down the barriers of separation; with increasing prosperity the mere shortage of white manpower will force the South African government to permit Africans to do jobs previously reserved for whites. This argument has been repeated ever since the National Party came into power and made 'separate development' an explicit doctrine, but in fact the trend of legislation has been steadily to intensify separation in every field. In housing, in employment, in every aspect of social life, the law has driven the races further apart; the violence with which the government daily enforces the law has grown more brutal. And it is small comfort to Africans to be told that, so long as there are not enough white men to fill all the jobs reserved exclusively for whites under the 'civilized labour policy', there is a chance of Africans being allowed to perform some of the worst paid and least skilled. Nor is it encouraging to tell them that 'in the end' industrial development must make for something different. What they suffer from is happening today and it is getting worse. In South Africa and Rhodesia the basic racial philosophy of those in power is more fundamental than economic considerations.[1]

Again, it is part of South Africa's foreign policy to establish with independent African nations a relationship that will at least encourage trade and permit diplomatic negotiation. This, it is argued, is bound to soften the rigidity of internal relations. But in fact to permit visiting African diplomats to stay at a specified white hotel need in no way interfere with the harsh operation of The Group Areas Act in general.

At one time, many of those who felt the injustice of the present situation hoped that it might be ended by the massive denial of African labour – a nation-wide general strike that would force the government to make concessions. It is no longer possible to regard anything of the kind as likely. Africans cannot be members of registered Trade Unions and any strike by Africans is illegal; the South African police and intelligence service are now outstandingly efficient. They have powers which enable them to detain anyone attempting to organize any action of this kind and they have no hesitation in using them. Even if such a movement could be planned and prepared – which now seems impossible – it would be likely to fail, partly because strikers could easily be cut off from food supplies and partly because a high proportion of the labour force is not South African. The 'foreign natives' (in the phraseology of South African administrators) are in the country to make money and go home; few of them are likely to accept the sacrifices that would be involved.

White people in South Africa who detest the system – and there are still many – must bring themselves to believe there is something to hope for. It is not surprising that they have clutched at arguments which have proved unrealistic. Visitors from Britain and America are less involved but are almost inevitably subjected to influences which are extremely misleading. They are bound to stay in white areas and with white people; they see Africans only as servants or workpeople and those they meet would be most unwise to confide in them. The most effective African leaders are in detention; the difficulties of meeting educated Africans who are prepared to express their opinions are extreme. Only white

[1] *Industrialization and Race Relations*, ed. Guy Hunter.

views are presented and it is tempting to be sympathetic to those which are optimistic. Both Britain and the United States have big investments in South Africa, Britain's being the greater absolutely and, proportionately to the national income, much the greater relatively. It is also convenient on strategic grounds to be friendly with South Africa. There is therefore every encouragement to the visitor to believe those who speak smooth things.

The strategic importance of South Africa is difficult to assess. There are those who argue that, in a nuclear war, it would be slight; on the other hand, there are undoubtedly still strong bodies of opinion which value the naval base at Simonstown. The controversy over the resumption of arms sales to South Africa has highlighted the arguments on both sides. So long as the Suez Canal is closed, South Africa is bound to count in the calculations of all who trade with South Asia. Both Britain and the USA would be reluctant to see the 'bastions' of South Africa strongly influenced by either Russia or China. On the whole, there can be little doubt that in British and American governmental eyes strategy reinforces investment as a motive for leaving South Africa alone. Indeed, such a policy is sometimes defended on the ground that an alliance gives powerful allies some influence over a weaker. But the argument has little force in questions of internal policy which the South African government regards as fundamental.

Massive political action by a combination of several powers seems the only practical means of cracking the Southern African fortress. But the two powers which could most effectively harm South Africa are Britain and the United States of America, the two which have most to lose. So far as force is concerned, Britain demonstrated her unwillingness to go to war over a matter of principle with Rhodesia; it is even less likely that such a risk would be taken in relation to South Africa, since it would involve a massive effort on a scale far greater than would be needed for Rhodesia.

It is important not to underestimate the difficulties of economic sanctions against South Africa. Britain's precarious balance of payments would be severely injured by the loss of trade with South Africa and neither major political party has so far shown any sign of readiness to face such a loss. Further, it is hard to suppose that other powers would not seek their own advantage if Britain and the United States were to refuse commercial relations.

Further, South Africa is in most respects self-sufficient, and has ample resources in coal, to which her industry is largely geared. She is less dependent on oil than most industrial nations and is well-stocked with oil. Further, supplies of oil have been discovered and dependence on foreign oil is bound to be reduced. To prevent oil from reaching South Africa would thus be of limited effectiveness even if achieved, and extremely difficult to achieve, it would mean the blockade of a long coastline with five ports widely spaced. It has been calculated that this would involve the use of aircraft carriers on a scale that only the United States could supply, and that would commit the US navy to the exclusion of any other active operations of any size elsewhere.

Nor would it be reasonable to pin hopes on the United Nations, which is subject to extreme financial trouble and reluctant to undertake fresh commitments after the lesson of the Congo. Since the decision on South-West Africa it has been hard for any African to see any hope in International Law or to regard the International Court of Justice as impartial. (See pages 23–4.)

The prospect of military success for the forces of change is perhaps greater in Angola and Mozambique than elsewhere in Southern Africa. Their long land frontiers with independent African states render them more open to guerilla infiltration.

Angola presents the tougher assignment to the guerillas. It is true that the savannah country in the north and east, with its wooded valleys and mountainous regions, is very suitable for guerilla warfare. On the other hand, the Congo and Zambia have proved rather insecure springboards for this kind of action, and are more sensitive to counter-pressures than (say) Tanzania. Angola's Portuguese army is readily supplied from Europe. Its growing settler population, its Atlantic outlook and increased investment from Europe and America have strengthened the Portuguese will to resist the rather unco-ordinated military designs of the different liberation movements.

In Mozambique, on the other hand, the northern provinces are no longer under effective Portuguese control. A more positive attitude on the part of Malawi would make the Tete salient difficult to hold, and this in turn could loosen Portugal's control over all the north. Greater unity among the African parties, the absence of a large hard-core settler population and the country's remoteness from Europe militate against final victory by the Portuguese.

The chief threat to Portugal from her African wars is, however, economic. The cost of maintaining 150,000 troops in Angola, Mozambique and Guinea distorts her own development and independence. Although the passing of Salazar has not brought any immediate change in overseas policy, the increasing pressure of the military effort in Africa is likely to increase unrest in Portugal itself. Without the economic and political support of Western allies, Portugal would probably already have had to come to terms with the new Africa.

In Rhodesia, white minority rule is firmly entrenched and policy is moving closer and closer to apartheid as known in South Africa. The two countries are becoming more closely linked economically and in social policies. There is no longer any hope of African constitutional advance, and despite Sir Alec Douglas Home's intention of making one more attempt on the basis of the Five Principles, prospects for successfully negotiating a just settlement between African and European are minimal. African leaders are aware of their deep predicament, as their fellows in South Africa have become. The activities of insurgents will trouble the country, and may slowly grow in significance. The growth in unemployment and rural poverty, the demands for education, and the growth of population, together with the changing ratio of African and white populations, will increase the fundamental pressures on the social and political system.

In the immediate future, then, we must conclude that throughout Southern Africa, except perhaps in Mozambique, there are in all human probability no signs of a substantial change in the position. The calculation of African revolutionaries that they have no peaceful means of redress appears to be justified. On the other hand, their use of force has no immediate prospect of success.

(ii) *What Christians should seek to achieve*

Many Christians will feel that it is not enough to conclude that the situation in Southern Africa is one of intolerable injustice and that in human probability nothing is likely to be done to put an end to it. They will feel that that is to commit the sin of despair. What is there for which Christians can hope and towards which they can work, even though they recognize that for the immediate future there are immense obstacles of human self-will in their way?

Five years ago a report to the British Council of Churches on South Africa was of the opinion that '*at the moment*' economic measures against South Africa were not advisable. But since then the situation has grown worse, the injustice more gross. We may be convinced that war against South Africa is impracticable. But can we believe it is right to accept economic interests as overriding all other considerations? Is it right that the British and American governments should refuse, in a just cause, to take any action that is economically harmful? We believe it is not. On the contrary, we believe it would be morally right, if we saw some practical means of achieving it, to impose total economic sanctions on South Africa and to enforce them by armed action against any vessels or aircraft that were in breach of the blockade. This, however, is altogether impracticable. It is therefore justifiable to pursue policies which are less satisfactory but also less impossible.

South Africa and Portugal have been the principal breakers of sanctions against Rhodesia. It would be reasonable strategy, therefore, to concentrate first on more attainable objects, and to work for an intensification of pressure on South Africa and Portugal to abandon their policy in this respect.

If the governments of the United Kingdom and the USA were agreed, and were determined on action, the following steps would be possible:

(i) Diplomatic pressure could be brought to bear on Portugal to stop breaking sanctions against Rhodesia. A first step would be to inform Portugal of our intention to recognize the freedom fighters as belligerents; this would make it legal to supply them with arms. If all NATO countries were agreed on this policy, pressure might include the threat of expulsion from the alliance and the cutting off of military supplies. Britain also could enforce important economic sanctions, including the stopping of the tourist trade. Diplomatic relations could also be reduced to the consular level. Such action would be very serious for Portugal.

Pressure of this kind, aimed at enforcing a resolution of the United Nations, might well tip the balance and persuade Portugal to change her whole policy and end the heavy commitment in lives and money which she is at present meeting in Africa. She could then look to a far more promising future in Europe.

(ii) At present, a resolution of the United Nations requests member nations not to supply arms to South Africa. The British Labour government accepted this resolution but interpreted it in such a way as to make it less than total. The plans of the present government are not yet clear, ~~but are likely to prove much less acceptable~~. If there was a true determination to do all in our power to bring about a change in Southern Africa, the ban on arms to South Africa would be total. There is no validity in the distinction between weapons used for internal security and those for defence against external aggression; it is safety against external aggression which permits the South African government to defy world opinion and use against their own people whatever weapons they find most convenient.

(iii) Again, if the determination existed, it would be possible to launch against South Africa the kind of propaganda campaign that we launched in war, by political speeches that would be widely reported, by the press and by broadcasting, which would include broadcasting in African languages.

(iv) Total economic blockade of South Africa is impracticable and anything less would have no chance of affecting South Africa's internal policy. But it might be possible by hard bargaining to achieve something, namely an end to sanctions-breaking. This could be stopped with comparatively little loss of face. The bargaining weapon for this might be – if determination existed – a ban on trade and investments as well as arms.

(v) Meanwhile the churches themselves could boycott firms with interests in South Africa.

The first four of these courses of action would stand a reasonable chance of success if our governments could be persuaded to adopt resolutely the objects we envisage. What Christians can – and indeed should – therefore do is to set about the persuasion of their people and governments.

5

Revolution, the Church and the Kingdom

The injustices and cruelties of government and society have too often gone unrebuked; revolution, and even change, have frequently been regarded purely negatively, and any attempt to overthrow 'lawful authority' has been condemned as positively sinful. There are understandable reasons for this. All human authority is fragile (as we are beginning once again to realize), good or even tolerable government is acknowledged to be a blessing, and almost any form of stable government has been found welcome by nations which have been through the experience of anarchy, at least until that experience has begun to fade from the popular memory. The burden of proof has therefore always rested on those who would disturb an existing order.

It is true that Christian theologians have often made allowance for the overthrow of tyranny; but it must be admitted that they and the churches have tended on the whole to weigh heavily in the opposite direction – particularly when the churches have been closely identified with the ruling power and still more, of course, when they have themselves claimed to be that power. In consequence, the prophetic tradition to which Jesus was heir has frequently been betrayed by organized Christianity, and the Christian rebel against injustice has often existed in spite of rather than in harmony with established religious authority. Too often it has been only when the secular power has turned against the church as an institution that the church has fought back. It has too often been reluctant to fight battles for others at its own expense – though its Master used force against the moneylenders but not for himself. On the other hand, the erring church has sometimes been 'rescued' by the dissenters within its own ranks.

So (to take an English example) it is to men like Wilberforce inspired by Christian principles that we attribute the success of the long struggle to end the slave trade: it is conveniently over-looked that because of the economic and social involvement of the Church of England with the power structures of the time, the bishops in the House of Lords voted to a man for the reten-tion of the *status quo*, i.e. the slave trade.

The twentieth century is seeing something like corporate penitence for this state of affairs emerging in what remains of Christendom. One of the signs of this readiness to rethink is the emergence of a 'theology of revolution', i.e. a readiness in many parts of the church to consider the relation between man's con-tinuing struggle for justice on earth and the teaching of Jesus about the Kingdom of God.

Here we must be clear about terminology. The struggle for justice in most societies means that there is a need for radical change. In some societies radical change can be achieved with-out revolution, that is without the violent overthrow not only of the government of the moment but of the whole structure of the society. We have tried to show that in Southern Africa the radi-cal change necessary for justice is not to be hoped for without revolution.

In this connection a caveat is necessary. If there is in some quarters today a genuine readiness to rethink Christian attitudes in the light of the needs of man and of the demands of the gospel, there is also some readiness for Christians to jump on currently popular secular band-wagons. It could even be argued, on grounds of prudence, that the church's best chance of survival in Latin America, and indeed in Southern Africa, is as an advo-cate of revolution. But such self-interest is unworthy of the gospel. To embrace revolution (and with it revolutionary vio-lence) on such grounds would be to display once again the cor-ruption of which the church has so often been guilty in the past; it would be to refuse to accept the implications of the Cross. On the other hand, if Christians accept involvement in a struggle for radical change out of deep conviction and at some real cost, this may well be a genuine expression of Christian discipleship.

The ethical discussion about the justification of revolutionary violence is concerned with both means and ends. But it is not a discussion that can be conducted dispassionately at a safe distance. It is a practical discussion by those who are actually prepared to struggle for liberation and to die in the process. Only where this readiness exists does the next question become relevant: am I also prepared to kill in the process? The answer of Gandhi, Luthuli, Luther King has been 'no'. This is the 'no' of the martyr. It is the genuine and legitimate 'no' of the disciple who knows and witnesses to the fact that an act which makes it impossible to love the enemy is an act of surrender to the enemy.

This ethic of total love in the struggle against every form of evil has never been corporately embraced by the church. Historically it has not been tried, politically it has not been put to the test. Given faith in it and limitless willingness to suffer, we do not seriously doubt the ultimate political effectiveness of such witness. In other words, if the majority or even a significant minority of non-whites in Southern Africa had faith to this degree and took their faith to its logical conclusion, we believe that apartheid could and would be destroyed, not, it is true, without the crucifixion of many on the road to victory, but probably with much less violence and suffering than that caused by the otherwise inevitable racial war. But since we know that sacrificial non-violence is only likely to be acceptable to rare individuals, we cannot accept it as a practical means of achieving an end. It is not the ethic of the white 'Christian' holders of power, who have brought their religion with them to Africa. And it would be blatant hypocrisy for wealthy, secure white churches in Southern Africa, which are non-pacifist and prepared to accept the moral possibility of armed violence in their own defence, to counsel oppressed peoples to turn the other cheek. On the other hand, a black 'Jesus' in South Africa today or tomorrow might well be crucified for telling his fellow Africans to do nothing inconsistent with loving even their worst oppressors. There would be no hypocrisy for him.

Similarly, it is impossible for a group of Christians in Britain to recommend sacrificial non-violence without being hypocritical. A body such as the British Council of Churches could not with consistency counsel others to non-violence while remaining ready to acknowledge the possibility of a 'just war' to defend Britain. If such a war can be just (and therefore theologically justifiable), then there can surely be no doubt about the justice of the revolutionary violence advocated as a last resort by the freedom fighters of Southern Africa.

So much for the question of principle. How about the question of effectiveness? In the present situation it would be right, and indeed a duty, to advocate non-violence as a method of obtaining revolutionary change, if it were believed that in practical ways non-violence might lead to the desired end. This would then be the advocacy of non-violence, not as a principle, but rather as a more effective means of achieving freedom. The issue at stake here is of the utmost importance because, if there is a way to obtain justice without revolutionary violence, then common sense, even shorn of ethical consideration, demands that that path be followed. History shows that violence is seldom a direct path to justice and to the establishment of a higher humanity.

This being so, there is a strong case for continuing study, both from within the countries we are considering and from without, of what methods short of all-out civil war might be used from within *and from outside* to break the power of the upholders of white supremacy in Southern Africa. From within the situation, all possible methods of non-violent action to obtain change have been tried (given people as they are) and have failed. On the other hand, it cannot be said that all possible methods of effecting change from outside have been tried. Of course, it can be assumed (and is perhaps assumed too readily) that people and governments being, collectively, what they are – self-centred and intent only on their own short-term interests – this line of approach, too, is illusory. Sanctions, many argue, are not worth struggling for because they will cost other nations (especially Britain) much more than they are willing to pay. That is not an argument against the desirability of effective sanctions. It is an argument for beginning a more effective movement in the economically powerful western nations – and in particular in Britain – to make an economic boycott of South Africa politically possible.

Having said all that, we recognize that for Christians the way of the Cross, the way of redemptive suffering, the determination to love at all costs remains *the* pattern of true discipleship. We believe that this way is the road to victory *for those who believe in it*. But for most men (inside as well as outside the church), the law rather than the gospel is the highest to which they have aspired. Thus, the ethics of the Old Testament prophets, while not the same as the ethics of Jesus, were, however, within their context and historical setting, an expression of the will of God. For most of us our social understanding of 'love' has not taken us beyond an understanding of elementary justice. And this is not to be despised in a world of bitter injustice and inhumanity.

It is on this basis that we believe that our churches should declare their solidarity with the *aims* of the revolution in Southern Africa and in comparable situations elsewhere. Revolution, even violent revolution, is in many parts of the world thought to be the only redress open to the oppressed. Of course to support their aims is not a way of turning guerilla warfare into a latter-day crusade or of deifying 'the revolution'. The individual freedom fighter may indeed be akin to a martyr, but if so, it will be for accepting the loss of his own life and in spite of what he is prepared to do to others. This has been well said by Archbishop Helder Camara of Recife, Brazil, from within such a situation:

> Let me say it naively and simply: I respect men who, driven by their conscience, decide to use violence – not the cheap violence of the drawing-room guerilla, but the violence of those who have testified to their sincerity by sacrificing their lives. It seems to me that Father Camillo Torres and Che Guevara deserve as much respect as Martin Luther King. Those whom I accuse are the real perpetrators of violence, those who, on the right and on the left, offend against justice and make peace impossible. For myself, I must go the way of a pilgrim of peace. I should much rather be killed than kill.

That is authentic witness from within the situation. If it is the Christian way, then the real respect from the 'pilgrim of peace' for the conscience of the revolutionary – the willingness to allow him to pursue justice in accord with his conscience – demands more than mere verbal respect. It demands active political, psychological and (perhaps most relevantly) financial support. This raises acute questions about the role of Christians in Britain in giving such support. To support the Defence and Aid Fund is not controversial among those who recognize the evils of apartheid. To facilitate the supply of arms for freedom fighters certainly is. Unless we can provide a better strategy for change, then we cannot both declare our solidarity with freedom fighters and refuse to help them. Verbal approval by the churches, however carefully phrased, would be better withheld if the practical consequences are ignored.

The profound spiritual conflict lies in deciding what means can be used to bring about political liberation without spiritual loss. The church cannot accept the naive assumption that the kingdom necessarily follows the overthrow of present injustice. The establishment of the kingdom in our midst demands more than revolutionary commitment. It demands unqualified love.

In all this the sincerity of Christians, both corporately and individually, is being judged by the way in which we act. This is why the report here presented faces the British churches with the difficult decision whether or not to accept an involvement with the revolutionary forces in Southern Africa. That in turn must mean that the church must be ready to see itself as an instrument of radical change (at home as well as abroad), and not merely as a moral arbiter over the conflicts of others. Neutrality is *de facto* support for the present injustices.

Only if the church is, and is seen to be, on the side of the revolution in Southern Africa, suffering and sharing in the guilt of spilt blood, can the church then, from within the situation, judge the revolution. This, like all human action, stands under judgment and foregiveness. Revolution inevitably involves suffering, death, separation and the ruin of human lives. Usually revolution has led to dictatorship, the establishment of a new tyranny. It seems likely that only a church within the revolution can help to humanize it. A church that is trapped into deifying revolution and making gods of its heroes has merely updated the pagan worship of war. To be within a revolution, and from there to speak prophetically to it, may be both illogical and terrifying. It is at this point that it may simply be necessary to be prepared to be foolish for Christ's sake. If the church merely became part of a revolutionary establishment, nothing would have been learnt.

Faith means that already, here and now, we must act on the

assumption that secular wisdom is not enough. We must seek freedom and justice within the circumstances as we understand them and we must do this in the name of him in whom anger and compassion became one at great cost.

6

Reflections and Recommendations Resulting from this Study

Summary

Britain's historical association with Southern Africa, and our strong links now, demand from churches in Britain a special concern for people there, and for our relations with the governments. The situation in Southern Africa concerns Christians all over the world, but *it is of special concern to us; our trade and our arms help to keep the situation as it is*.

Southern Africa must be considered as a whole; conditions in one area interact with those in the remainder. Peace will not be achieved until there is peace for the whole.

In the five territories considered in this report, the majority of the inhabitants have been generally dispossessed of their land and placed in an inferior position in society; racial discrimination and injustice have been legalized. These experiences lie deeply in the memories of the repressed people today, who see no possibility of changing their situation by constitutional processes. *Society in these five territories is manifestly unjust*, not only by the standards that Christians would apply as a result of their allegiance to Jesus Christ, but also by the standards generally accepted in the contemporary world, for example by the ~~UN Charter~~ Universal Declaration of Human Rights. *The list of human rights in the Charter is a list of what Africans may not do in South Africa.*

The ways of reconciliation must continue to be tried, but it must be recognized that peaceful means have been attempted by the oppressed people and so far have failed. Similarly, international persuasion has failed; international police action has not been tried. These failures leave the dispossessed with no alternative to complete subjection except to attempt liberation themselves. In the circumstances of Southern Africa, peaceful demonstration and withdrawal of labour offer little hope of peaceful advancement in the securing of basic human rights. *Unconstitutional action is the only course left open.*

The stage when liberal political measures would have met the immediate aspirations of the people has passed. *Radical change in political control is now demanded.*

The necessary changes will not come, we believe, from economic and population pressures. These have so far produced only an intensification of oppression. *It is therefore right for Christians both within and without Southern Africa to advocate fundamental political and social change*

The emergence of liberation movements arises from a prolonged period of mounting oppression. Many Christians within those movements, including some of the leaders, are acting to remedy the injustices suffered by their fellow men. They are aware of the deep moral dilemmas posed by their action. With some there is profound disillusion with the Christian church, because of its complacency in the face of injustice; others retain an attitude of respect for the traditional separation of the churches from direct political involvement.

Militant action by the resistance movements has the sympathy of many of the people. So long as the present conditions continue there is likely to be a continual growth of violent resistance, which may be expected to be a feature of Southern Africa for many years. *But in the short term, there is very limited prospect of success.*

In these states, force is controlled by a minority, to preserve the privileged position of that minority. Force must be present in all societies, but for the protection of the rights of all the people, not to maintain the privilege of a few at the expense of the many; it should be held in reserve, used occasionally and to control occasional dissidents. There it is used habitually and to control the majority of the population. *It is a falsehood to claim that it is used to defend 'Christian civilization'.*

We are well aware that armed resistance to a government involves inescapable suffering for many people and the apparent ruin of many lives. In spite of the great moral difficulties, fighting for a just cause has been generally accepted by the Christian conscience as justifiable if certain conditions are fulfilled. The action of those in rebellion, as of those at war, must be subject to moral judgment, both as to means and as to objects. Those who are themselves in comfort and security cannot urge armed rebellion on others who would thereby face death or life imprisonment. Nor can they preach patient endurance of a suffering they do not have to bear. *But there can be a just rebellion as well as a just war and we cannot sincerely withhold support from those who have decided to face the certain suffering involved in such rebellion.*

Considerations for Christians in Britain

As a result of their study and discussion, the Working Party have reached the following basic conclusions:

It is too late to insist that our support should be confined to those pledged to non-violence. To urge their subjects to avoid violence furthers the ends of the governments of these five territories, who themselves habitually employ violence to repress any move that would upset the rule of privileged minorities. *The time has come to show our solidarity with those seeking radical change and struggling for freedom in Southern Africa.*

At the same time we should understand their convictions and give support to those Christians in Southern Africa who are pledged to non-violence.

From these basic conclusions, there follow certain courses of action open to Christians in Britain.

We believe that it is the duty of Christians in Britain to study the situation in Southern Africa, to use imagination to understand what it means in the lives of human beings, to bring to light the injustices which many people are suffering, to communicate what they have learnt and understood to others, and to persuade a wider public of the need for action. This involves a long-term programme of education.

We further believe that:

Christians should lose no chance of bringing home to the people of the United Kingdom the evils of a repressive system of government based on distinctions of colour. Of this the supreme example is the South African. Churches and individuals should maintain pressure on our government and on members of parliament to show a practical concern about the situation in Southern Africa by such courses of action as are set out on pages 65–67 of this report, including a total embargo on arms and pressure to end the breach of economic sanctions against Rhodesia.

This must not obscure their perception of the acute dilemma in which white South Africans are placed, nor their concern for their safety and future. But justice to the Africans must come before the comfort and convenience of whites.

The widespread and permanent system of migrant labour, in all the territories under consideration, causes grave problems for the community and for families. The churches need to study the issues and to use all their influence against this system.

Christians should understand what it means to be an exile. Opportunities should be taken to give assistance and care to the families of those engaged in resistance, to refugees and to those in detention.

Relief and voluntary service organizations (including Christian Youth organizations) should include in their operations raising funds for refugee rehabilitation and development aspects of liberation movements. Some organizations can assist in community training and scholarship programmes. Aid can be channelled through responsible liaison committees.

Churches and missionary societies should be prepared to help in every way, but particularly with finance and personnel for development purposes, in territories where liberation movements may establish control. Support may be given to create community services and to advance the livelihood of the people.

Individual Christians who accept the argument of the Working Party that rebellion in Southern Africa is justified have many courses open, depending on their personal circumstances and individual consciences. Some may wish to collect funds for freedom fighters without conditions; others will prefer to confine themselves to funds of the kind mentioned in the previous paragraphs; others again will find their degree of commitment leads them to other courses of action. The one attitude that is not defensible is indifference.

We are aware that some will find our views distressing. But silence and smooth words have been responsible for the long failure to understand what is happening and have permitted an indecision which is a reproach to Christians in Britain. We believe that failure to speak out now would be dishonest. The injustices of which we have written are glaring; the need to act is urgent.

The conflict over race is world-wide; we cannot isolate the pain nor the protest. Already in our own country we see the growth of fear and prejudice. But this is no excuse for inaction in respect of Southern Africa; on the contrary, we cannot honestly combat prejudice in Britain, still less deal with it successfully, unless we take a firm stand on Southern Africa. Nor can we ease our consciences by indignation about apartheid unless we are active against discrimination here. In this matter, there is a clear choice between right and wrong which knows no national boundaries.

With humility and penitence, we urge this country to range itself on the side of Christian teaching, of humanity, of justice.

Rhodesia: Joint Pastoral Letter on the New Constitution

The following letter was issued by the Roman Catholic Bishops in Rhodesia, before the Referendum of June 20th, 1969. The electorate, predominantly European, gave approval to the constitutional proposals, and the 1969 Constitution based on them was later adopted. This is one of several pronouncements by Catholic and Protestant church leaders, clearly opposing constitutional development and legislation such as the Land Tenure Act.

Two years ago the people of Rhodesia were asked to submit proposals for a new Constitution. We, the Catholic Bishops, availed ourselves of the opportunity and presented to the Whaley Commission carefully prepared suggestions designed to ensure that this Constitution should promote the common good, guarantee the dignity and the freedom of every individual, build up a true social order, bring about the unity of the nation, and establish concord with other nations.

In our examination of the proposals recently published we have kept in mind not only our duty to preserve and promote the moral order but the duty also of all our people likewise to promote the moral order and act in accordance with it. It is a responsibility which rests on everyone irrespective of race.

We have brought to bear on our examination of the text of the Proposals our considerable experience of Rhodesian life and our knowledge of all its people. We have remembered the non-African minority who have contributed so greatly to the country's development and whose interests, like those of any other group, must at all times be protected from undue interference. We have thought no less of the majority, the African people, of whom we have a particular knowledge, whose well-being as the weaker group we are in charity bound vigilantly to care for and whose friendship we are in a special way privileged to enjoy.

We are fully aware of the seriousness of the step we take when we say that the Proposals for the new Constitution are in many respects completely contrary to Christian teaching and we must therefore reject them and, for the benefit of our own people and of all men of good-will, publicly condemn them.

The spirit of justice and fraternal charity which is at the heart of all our Divine Lord's teaching finds no place in the document. His command to do unto others as we would have them do unto us (Matt. 7.12) is outlawed in these Proposals which have clearly been drafted not with the purpose of achieving the common good, but with the deliberate intent of ensuring the permanent domination of one section of the population over the other, in such a way that practices of racial discrimination shall be intensified and the unwarranted privileges of one group consolidated at the expense of the other.

Such policy is quite irreconcilable with God's law and in time to come must have the most tragic consequences for the country as a whole. We cannot be silent when a moral issue of such extreme gravity is in question. The Church has the right to pass moral judgment even on matters touching the political order whenever personal basic rights or the salvation of souls make such judgment necessary.

We note with particular concern the following points in the Constitutional Proposals:

(a) On moral grounds we vehemently protest against the powers to be conceded to the Administration. In virtue of such powers, discriminatory executive and administrative acts would be excluded from the Declaration of Human Rights and indeed removed from even the limited censure of the Senate. To accept such powers as being constitutional would be morally unjustifiable. It would be the equivalent of signing a blank cheque for government by bureaucratic dictatorship.

(b) Whereas we had urged that there should be a specific Declaration of Rights and an independent body created for the

maintenance of the spirit as well as the letter of this Declaration, in the Proposals these basic human rights are not
described clearly and unequivocally and are declared to be
non-justifiable. If these proposals are implemented, no
court would 'have the right to enquire into, or pronounce
upon, the validity of any law on the ground that it is inconsistent with the Declaration of Rights'. (Section 38,
Part One: Proposals for a New Constitution for Rhodesia).
The guardianship of the Declaration would be taken away
from the Constitutional Council and exercised by the
Senate, an organ of government which is not immune
from political pressures. This is most undesirable as it
would pave the way for the encroachment of government
on the rights of the individual.

(c) We are most seriously concerned at the limitations which
in terms of the Proposals could be imposed on the rights
of freedom of expression. This could mean that the voice
of the people could be silenced by government decree, the
teaching mission of the Church gravely impeded and the
means of communication perverted into becoming the
brainwashing instruments of any dictatorial regime.

(d) The new Constitution will not provide adequate elected
representation for all sections of the population. Instead,
a small minority will for an unforeseeable time to come
have a two-thirds majority in the House of Assembly.
Further, a new criterion of representation, defective in
equity and contrary to the fundamental principles of social
justice, has been introduced, in that Africans in the House
of Assembly are to be represented in proportion to their
collective income-tax assessment. This oft-proclaimed
principle of advancement on merit is thus set aside in
favour of government by group, a man's worth and responsibility being estimated according to his wealth.

(e) In previous pastoral statements we have made clear beyond all doubt our conscientious objection to laws which
segregate people merely on the basis of race. The new
Constitutional Proposals with their separate rolls and con-
stituencies to be determined solely on the basis of race
are therefore wholly unacceptable to us, as are also the

proposed provisions for Land Tenure, which are obviously intended to render difficult any real unification of the nation.

(f) A further deplorable aspect of the new Proposals is that they favour the perpetuation and indeed the increase of tribalism. Representation in Parliament according to tribal origins and the establishment of Provincial Councils for other than purely administrative purposes militate against the possibility of ever building a single Rhodesian nation.

The divisive and disruptive elements contained in these Proposals are not only irreconcilable with the Christian spirit of brotherhood and with the civil duty of promoting national unity, they are calculated to destroy every possibility of achieving the common good. No one should be deceived by them. They offer a superficial but completely illusory hope of security for the future, and can only breed hatred and violence. If they should be implemented in a new Constitution, it will be extremely difficult for us effectively to counsel moderation to a people who have been patient for so long under discriminatory laws and are now presented with such extreme provocation.

It is not by Proposals such as these that the traditional understanding and friendship between races can be retained and the future of Rhodesia assured. Only even-handed justice and conduct enlightened by Christian charity can give this or any other country real hope of stability, progress and peace, or enable it to establish lasting concord with other nations.

It should be clear, therefore, that no one may hold himself free from blame if in this momentous matter he should neglect to vote, or cast his vote without thoroughly informing himself of what is at issue and making his decision before God and his conscience.

Signed by: The Most Rev. Francis Markall, S.J., Archbishop of Salisbury.

The Right Reverend A. Haene, S.M.B., Bishop of Gwelo.

The Right Reverend A. G. Schmitt, C.M.M., Bishop of Bulawayo.

The Right Reverend D. R. Lamont, O.Carm.,
Bishop of Umtali.
The Right Reverend Ignatius Prieto Vega, S.M.I.,
Bishop of Wankie.

(*Fides, June 14, 1969*)

Appendix II

A Message to The People of South Africa

The 'Message' was published in 1969 by the South African Council of Churches. It was the work of a Theological Commission appointed by the Council and was offered to Christians for study. Individuals were invited to sign the document as an expression of Christian commitment.

It is valuable as an indication of how some Christians in South Africa are thinking about their faith. At the same time, it has to be remembered that many resolutions and statements have been made by Christian bodies, over many years, but the impact on the total situation has been slight.

This is a summary of the 'Message', authorized by the Council of Churches:

In the name of Jesus Christ:

We are under an obligation to confess anew our commitment to the universal faith of Christians, the eternal Gospel of salvation and security in Christ alone.

The Gospel of Jesus Christ is the good news that in Christ God has broken down the walls of division between God and man, and between man and man.

The Gospel of Jesus Christ declares that Christ is the truth who sets men free from all false hopes of freedom and security.

The Gospel of Jesus Christ declares that God has shown himself as the conqueror of all the forces that threaten to separate and isolate and destroy us.

The Gospel of Jesus Christ declares that God is reconciling us to himself and to each other; and that therefore such barriers as race and nationality have no rightful place in the inclusive brotherhood of Christian disciples.

The Gospel of Jesus Christ declares that God is the master of this world, and that it is to him alone that we owe our primary commitment.

The Gospel of Jesus Christ declares that the Kingdom of God is already present in Christ, demanding our obedience and our faith now.

This Gospel of Jesus Christ offers hope and security for the whole life of man, not just in man's spiritual and ecclesiastic relationships, but for human existence in its entirety. Consequently, we are called to witness to the meaning of the Gospel in the particular circumstances of time and place in which we find ourselves. In South Africa, at this time, we find ourselves in a situation where a policy of racial separation is being deliberately effected with increasing rigidity. The doctrine of racial separation is being seen by many not merely as a temporary political policy but as a necessary and permanent expression of the will of God, and as the genuine form of Christian obedience for this country. It is holding out to men a security built not on Christ but on the theory of separation and the preservation of racial identity; it is presenting the separate development of our race-groups as the way for the people of South Africa to save themselves. And this claim is being made to us in the name of Christianity.

We believe that this doctrine of separation is a false faith, a novel gospel. It inevitably is in conflict with the Gospel of Jesus Christ, which offers salvation, both individual and social, through faith in Christ alone. It is keeping people away from the real knowledge of Christ; therefore it is the Church's duty to enable our people to distinguish between the demands of the South African state and the demands of Christian discipleship.

The Christian Gospel requires us to assert the truth proclaimed by the first Christians, who discovered that God was creating a new community in which differences of race, language, nation, culture and tradition no longer had power to separate man from man. The most important features of a man are not the details of his racial group, but the nature which he has in common with all man and also the gifts and abilities which are given to him as a unique individual by the grace of God; to insist that racial characteristics are more important than these is to reject what is most significant about our own humanity as well as the humanity of others.

But, in South Africa, everyone is expected to believe that a man's racial identity is the most important thing about him; only when it is clearly settled can any significant decisions be made about him. Those whose racial classification is in any doubt are tragically insecure and helpless. Without racial identity, it seems, we can do nothing; he who has it, has life, he who has not racial identity has not life. This belief in the supreme importance of racial identity amounts to a denial of the central statements of the Christian Gospel. In practice, it severely restricts the ability of Christians brothers to serve and to know each other, and even to give each other simple hospitality; it limits the ability of a person to obey Christ's command to love his neighbour as himself. For, according to the Christian Gospel, our brothers are not merely members of our own race-group. Our brother is the person whom God gives to us. To dissociate from our brother on the grounds of natural distinction is to despise God's gift and to reject Christ.

Where different groups of people are hostile to each other, this is due to human sin, not to the plan of the Creator. The Scriptures do not require such groups to be kept separate from each other; on the contrary, the Gospel requires us to believe in and to act on the reconciliation made for us in Christ. A policy of separation is a demonstration of unbelief in the power of the Gospel; any demonstration of the reality of reconciliation would endanger this policy. Therefore, the advocates of this policy inevitably find themselves opposed to the Church if it seeks to live according to the Gospel and to show that God's grace has overcome our hostilities. A thorough policy of racial separation must ultimately require that the Church should cease to be the Church.

The Gospel of Jesus Christ declares that God is love; separation is the opposite force of love. The Christian Gospel declares that separation is the supreme threat and danger, but that in Christ it has been overcome; it is in association with Christ and with each other that we find our true identity. But apartheid is a view of life and of man which insists that we find our identity in dissociation and distinction from each other; it rejects as undesirable the reconciliation which God is giving to us by his Son; it reinforces distinctions which the Holy Spirit is calling the people of God to overcome; it calls good evil. This policy is, therefore, a form of resistance to the Holy Spirit.

The Gospel of Jesus Christ declares that Christ is our master, and that to him all authority is given. Christians betray their calling if they give their highest loyalty, which is due to Christ alone, to one group or tradition, especially where that group is demanding self-expression at the expense of other groups. God judges us, not by our loyalty to a sectional group but by our willingness to be made new in the community of Christ. Christ is inevitably a threat to much that is called 'the South African way of life'; many features of our social order will have to pass away if the lordship of Christ is to be truly acknowledged and if the peace of Christ is to be revealed as the destroyer of our fear.

And Christ is master of the Church also. If the Church fails to witness to the true Gospel of Jesus Christ it will find itself witnessing to a false gospel. If we seek to reconcile Christianity with the so-called 'South African way of life' we shall find that we have allowed an idol to take the place of Christ. Where the Church abandons its obedience to Jesus Christ, it ceases to be the Church; it breaks the links between itself and the Kingdom of God. The task of the Church is to enable people to see the power of God at work, changing hostility into love of the brethren, and to express God's reconciliation here and now. For we are not required to wait for a distant 'heaven' where all problems will have been solved. What Christ has done, he has done already. We can accept his work or reject it; we can hide from it or seek to live by it. But we cannot postpone it, for it is already achieved, and we cannot destroy it, for it is the work of the eternal God.

We believe that Christ is the Lord, and that South Africa is part of his world. We believe that his Kingdom and its righteousness have power to cast out all that opposes his purposes and keeps men in darkness. We believe that the word of God is not bound, and that it will move with power in these days, whether men hear or whether they refuse to hear. And so we wish to put to every Christian person in the country the question which we ourselves face each day; to whom, or to what, are you giving your first loyalty, your primary commitment? Is it to be a sub-section of mankind, an ethnic group, a human tradition, a political idea; or to Christ?

May God enable us to be faithful to the Gospel of Jesus Christ, and to be committed to Christ alone!

The Rivonia Trial: South Africa

In connection with the sentences in the Rivonia trial[1], a statement issued by Chief Albert J. Luthuli on 12th June, 1964 deserves attention:

> Sentences of life imprisonment have been pronounced on Nelson Mandela, Walter Sisulu, Ahmed Kathrada, Govan Mbeki, Dennis Goldberg, Raymond Mhlaba, Elias Motsoaledi and Andrew Mlangeni in the Rivonia Trial in Pretoria.
>
> Over the long years these leaders advocated a policy of racial co-operation, of goodwill, and of peaceful struggle that made the South African liberation movement one of the most ethical and responsible of our time. In the face of the most bitter racial persecution, they resolutely set themselves against racialism; in the face of continued provocation, they consistently chose the path of reason.
>
> The African National Congress, with allied organizations representing all racial sections, sought every possible means of redress for intolerable conditions and held consistently to a policy of using militant, non-violent means of struggle. Their common aim was to create a South Africa in which all South Africans would live and work together as fellow-citizens, enjoying equal rights without discrimination on grounds of race, colour or creed.
>
> To this end, they used every accepted method: propaganda, public meetings and rallies, petitions, stay-at-home-strikes, appeals, boycotts. So carefully did they educate the people that in the four-year-long Treason Trial, one police witness

[1] See UN Unit on Apartheid: 13/69.

after another voluntarily testified to this emphasis on non-violent methods of struggle in all aspects of their activities.

But finally all avenues of resistance were closed. The African National Congress and other organizations were made illegal; their leaders jailed, exiled or forced underground. The government sharpened its oppression of the peoples of South Africa, using its all-White parliament as the vehicle for making repression legal, and utilizing every weapon of this highly industrialized and modern state to enforce that 'legality'. The stage was even reached where a White spokesman for the disenfranchised Africans was regarded by the government as a traitor. In addition, sporadic acts of uncontrolled violence were increasing throughout the country. At first in one place and then in another, there were spontaneous eruptions against intolerable conditions, many of these acts increasingly assumed a racial character.

The African National Congress never abandoned its method of a militant, non-violent struggle, and of creating in the process a spirit of militancy in the people. However, in the face of the uncompromising White refusal to abandon a policy which denies the African and other oppressed South Africans their rightful heritage – freedom – no one can blame brave men for seeking justice by the use of violent methods; nor could they be blamed if they tried to create an organized force in order to ultimately establish peace and racial harmony.

For this, they are sentenced to be shut away for long years in the brutal and degrading prisons of South Africa. With them will be interred this country's hopes of racial co-operation. They will leave a vacuum in leadership that may only be filled by bitter hate and racial strife.

They represent the highest in morality and ethics in the South African political struggle; this morality and ethics have been sentenced to an imprisonment it may never survive. Their policies are in accordance with the deepest international principles of brotherhood and humanity; without their leadership, brotherhood and humanity may be blasted out of existence and reason; when they are locked away, justice and reason will have departed from the South African scene.

This is an appeal to save these men, not merely as individuals, but for what they stand for. In the name of justice, of hope, of truth and of peace, I appeal to South Africa's strongest allies, Britain and America. In the name of what we have come to believe Britain and America stand for, I appeal to those two powerful countries to take decisive action for full-scale sanctions that would precipitate the end of the hateful system of apartheid.

I appeal to all governments throughout the world, to people everywhere, to organizations and institutions in every land and at every level, to act now to impose such sanctions on South Africa that will bring about the vital necessary change and avert what can become the greatest African tragedy of our times.

The Archbishop of Canterbury, Dr Ramsey, commented as follows on the convictions and sentences:

The men were guilty of sabotage and other offences against the law as it exists, but their actions were the outcome of conscience, and wherever in the world there is respect for conscience and hatred of the policy of apartheid, there will be understanding of Mr Mandela's words that he acted from 'a calm and sober assessment of the situation after many years of oppression and tyranny of my people by the Whites'. If he is guilty before the existing law, the guilt before heaven belongs to the policy which the law is designed to enforce. The ideal and practice of apartheid is a denial of God's law of the relation of man to man as, irrespective of colour, created in the image of God.

Twelve Statements for the Consideration of all Christian
Voters in the Republic of South Africa

This document was issued before the General Election in April
1970 in South Africa, over the signature of seventy-two church
leaders. The supporters included Archbishop Robert S. Taylor,
Revs. C. F. B. Naudé, B. Moore, A. Boraine, Dale White, Rt.
Rev. P. W. R. Russell, Rt. Rev. C. Winter, Fr. C. Collins and
Dr E. H. Brookes.

Many church leaders and Christian educationalists were invited to sign the document but refused to do so.

1. Every Christian has an inescapable responsibility, especially
   he who has the vote.

2. Politics concerns itself with the arrangement of society and
   therefore most intimately affects the lives of people created
   in the image of God.

3. It is the Christian's duty to contribute by his vote towards
   the establishment of a government which shall promote law
   and order, and shall work for the welfare of the whole community over which it is appointed, in accordance with the
   Biblical commandments of truth, justice and love.

4. Any arrangement of a people's life which is not in accordance with the commandments of truth, justice and love opposes the common good, endangers law and order, conflicts
   with the will of God and therefore leads to the downfall of
   such a people.

5. In his acts of creation and of salvation, God reveals that He
   is deeply concerned about human society as well as about

the life and fate of every individual. This is why the Christian recognizes the intrinsic value of society, and the dignity of every individual.

6. The Christian shares in the responsibility for the arrangement of society in accordance with the revealed commandments and promises of God. Hence, in his political witness and action, he should be obedient to the revealed will of God and reject anything which conflicts with it.

7. Every Christian must, therefore, give account to God concerning his giving or withholding of support for any particular political party and its policy. He should test his own participation in politics by the following basic standards.

8. *Reconciliation*. In obedience to God, no Christian can support a political policy which is based on an unjust discrimination, on arbitrary grounds of colour, race, religion or sex, between people who live and work in the same country. He must further reject such a policy of discrimination when it leads to a consistent enforced separation of such people without their common consent. Man's sinful urge towards discrimination and separation stands in direct conflict with the Bible's message of reconciliation.

9. *Truth*. In obedience to God, no Christian can support a political policy which, being demonstrably impracticable, bases its appeal to the electorate on false claims and promises. Such an essentially dishonest policy cannot be reconciled with the Christian's commitment to the truth.

10. *Justice*. In obedience to God, no Christian can support a political policy which, for its practical implementation, unavoidably necessitates open or concealed injustice towards any individual or population group. A policy which essentially diminishes, offends or injures the human dignity of any citizen, must be totally rejected by the Christian.

11. *Love*. In obedience to God, no Christian can support a political policy which is essentially based on group selfishness and the furtherance of sectional interests only. Such a policy leads to inhumanity and lovelessness and must consequently clash with the law of love given by Christ.

12. It is the Christian's grave duty and responsibility thoroughly to examine the policy of every political party in South Africa and to acquaint himself with its implications. He must weigh all political utterances and policies against the truth of God. In so doing he may find that no available political policy represents complete obedience to this truth; he will nevertheless be obliged, in making his judgment, to approach as closely as possible to a complete obedience.

The Christian who has the vote must guard against the temptation to make decisions based on personal or group selfishness. His responsibility becomes even greater in a society where a small minority of citizens elect the members of the central parliament.

In short, the Christian's participation in politics must be determined by his inescapable responsibility towards God and his neighbour.

Signed by seventy-two church leaders
January, 1970

Appendix V

The Future of Southern Africa

This manifesto was issued during a conference of fourteen heads of state, foreign ministers or their representatives, at Lusaka in April, 1970. Those present included Mr Kenneth Kaunda, Mr Julius Nyerere, and ministers from Ethiopia, Kenya, Rwanda, Congo (Brazzaville), Congo (Kinshasa), Somalia, Burundi, Central African Republic, Sudan, Chad, Uganda. It is an important presentation of the political attitudes of states in East and Central Africa. It has not received recognition or reply from the countries of Southern Africa.

1. When the purpose and the basis of States' international policies are misunderstood, there is introduced into the world a new and unnecessary disharmony. Disagreements, conflicts of interest, or different assessments of human priorities, which already provoke an excess of tension in the world, and disastrously divide mankind at a time when united action is necessary to control modern technology and put it to the service of man. It is for this reason that discovering widespread misapprehension of our attitudes and purpose in relation to Southern Africa, we the leaders of East and Central African States meeting at Lusaka, 16th April, 1969, have agreed to issue this Manifesto.

2. By this Manifesto we wish to make clear, beyond all shadow of doubt, our acceptance of the belief that all men are equal, and have equal rights to human dignity and respect, regardless of colour, race, religion or sex. We believe that all men have the right and the duty to participate as equal members of the society, in their own government. We do not accept

that any individual or group has any right to govern any other group of sane adults, without their consent, and we affirm that only the people of a society, acting together as equals, can determine what is, for them, a good society and a good social, economic or political organization.

3. On the basis of these beliefs we do not accept that any one group within a society has the right to rule any society without the continuing consent of all the citizens. We recognize that at any one time there will be, within every society, failures in the implementation of these ideals. We recognize that for the sake of order in human affairs there may be transitional arrangements while a transformation from group inequalities to individual equality is being effected. But we affirm that without an acceptance of these ideals – without a commitment to these principles of human equality and self-determination – there can be no basis for peace and justice in the world.

4. None of us would claim that within our own States we have achieved that perfect social, economic and political organization which would ensure a reasonable standard of living for all our people and establish individual security against avoidable hardship or miscarriage of justice. On the contrary, we acknowledge that within our own States the struggle towards human brotherhood and unchallenged human dignity is only beginning. It is on the basis of our commitment to human equality and human dignity, not on the basis of achieved perfection, that we take our stand of hostility towards the colonialism and racial discrimination which is being practised in Southern Africa. It is on the basis of their commitment to these universal principles that we appeal to other members of the human race for support.

5. If the commitment to these principles existed among the States holding power in Southern Africa, any disagreements we might have about the rate of implementation, or about isolated acts of policy, would be matters affecting only our individual relationships with the States concerned. If these commitments existed, our States would not be justified in the expressed and active hostility towards the regimes of

Southern Africa such as we have proclaimed and continue to propagate.

6. The truth is, however, that in Mozambique, Angola, Rhodesia, South-West Africa, and the Republic of South Africa, there is an open and continued denial of the principles of human equality and national self-determination. This is not a matter of failure in the implementation of accepted human principles. The effective Administrations in all these territories are not struggling towards these difficult goals. They are fighting the principles; they are deliberately organizing their societies so as to try to destroy the hold of these principles in the minds of men. It is for this reason that we believe the rest of the world must be interested. For the principle of human equality, and all that flows from it, is either universal or it does not exist. The dignity of all men is destroyed when the manhood of any human being is denied.

7. Our objectives in Southern Africa stem from our commitment to this principle of human equality. We are not hostile to the Administration of these States, because they are manned and controlled by white people. We are hostile to them because they are systems of minority control which exist as a result of, and in the pursuance of, doctrines of human inequality. What we are working for is the right of self-determination for the people of those territories. We are working for a rule in those countries which is based on the will of all the people, and an acceptance of the equality of every citizen.

8. Our stand towards Southern Africa thus involves a rejection of racialism, not a reversal of the existing racial domination. We believe that all the peoples who have made their homes in the countries of Southern Africa are Africans, regardless of the colour of their skins; and we would oppose a racialist majority government which adopted a philosophy of deliberate and permanent discrimination between its citizens on grounds of racial origin. We are not talking racialism when we reject the colonialism and apartheid policies now operating in those areas; we are demanding an opportunity for all

the people of these States, working together as equal individual citizens, to work out for themselves the institutions and the system of government under which they will, by general consent, live together and work together to build a harmonious society.

9. As an aftermath of the present policies it is likely that different groups within these societies will be self-conscious and fearful. The initial political and economic organizations may well take account of these fears, and this group self-consciousness. But how this is to be done must be a matter exclusively for the peoples of the country concerned, working together. No other nation will have a right to interfere in such affairs. All that the rest of the world has a right to demand is just what we are now asserting – that the arrangements within any State which wishes to be accepted into the community of nations must be based on an acceptance of the principles of human dignity and equality.

10. To talk of the liberation of Africa is thus to say two things: First, that the peoples in the territories still under colonial rule shall be free to determine for themselves their own institutions of self-government. Secondly, that the individuals in Southern Africa shall be freed from an environment poisoned by the propaganda of racialism, and given an opportunity to be men – not white men, brown men, yellow men, or black men.

11. Thus the liberation of Africa for which we are struggling does not mean a reverse racialism. Nor is it an aspect of African Imperialism. As far as we are concerned the present boundaries of the States of Southern Africa are the boundaries of what will be free and independent African States. There is no question of our seeking or accepting any alterations to our own boundaries at the expense of these future free African nations.

12. On the objective of liberation, as thus defined, we can neither surrender nor compromise. We have always preferred and still prefer, to achieve it without physical violence. We would prefer to negotiate rather than destroy, to talk rather than kill. We do not advocate violence; we advocate an end

to the violence against human dignity which is now being perpetrated by the oppressors of Africa. If peaceful progress to emancipation were possible, or if changed circumstances were to make it possible in the future, we would urge our brothers in the resistance movements to use peaceful methods of struggle even at the cost of some compromise on the timing of change. But while peaceful progress is blocked by actions of those at present in power in the States of Southern Africa, we have no choice but to give to the peoples of those territories all the support of which we are capable in their struggle against their oppressors. This is why the signatory states participate in the movement for the liberation of Africa, under the aegis of the Organization of African Unity. However, the obstacle to change is not the same in all the countries in Southern Africa, and it follows, therefore, that the possibility of continuing the struggle through peaceful means varies from one country to another.

13. In *Mozambique* and *Angola*, and in so-called *Portuguese Guinea*, the basic problem is not racialism but a pretence that Portugal exists in Africa. Portugal is situated in Europe; the fact that it is a dictatorship is a matter for the Portuguese to settle. But no decree of the Portuguese dictator, nor legislation passed by any Parliament in Portugal, can make Africa part of Europe. The only thing which could convert a part of Africa into a constituent unit in a union which also includes a European State would be the freely expressed will of the people of that part of Africa. There is no such popular will in the Portuguese colonies. On the contrary, in the absence of any opportunity to negotiate a road to freedom, the peoples of all three territories have taken up arms against the colonial power. They have done this despite the heavy odds against them, and despite the great suffering they know to be involved.

14. Portugal, as a European State, has naturally its own allies in the context of the ideological conflict between West and East. However, in our context the effect of this is that Portugal is enabled to use her resources, to pursue the most

heinous war and degradation of man in Africa. The present Manifesto must, therefore, lay bare the fact that the in-human commitment of Portugal in Africa and her ruthless subjugation of the people of Mozambique, Angola and the so-called Portuguese Guinea, is not only irrelevant to the ideological conflict of power-politics, but it is also diametric-ally opposed to the politics, the philosophies and the doc-trines practised by her Allies in the conduct of their own affairs at home. The peoples of Mozambique, Angola and Portuguese Guinea are not interested in Communism or Capitalism; they are interested in their freedom. They are demanding an acceptance of the principles of independence on the basis of majority rule, and for many years they called for discussions on this issue. Only when their demand for talks was continually ignored did they begin to fight. Even now, if Portugal should change her policy and accept the principle of self-determination we would urge the liberation movements to desist from their armed struggle and to co-operate in the mechanics of a peaceful transfer of power from Portugal to the peoples of the African territories.

15. The fact that many Portuguese citizens have immigrated to these African countries does not affect this issue. Future immigration policy will be a matter for the independent governments when these are established. In the meantime we would urge the Liberation Movements to reiterate their statements that all those Portuguese people who have made their homes in Mozambique, Angola, or Portuguese Guinea, and who are willing to give their future loyalty to those States, will be accepted as citizens. And an independent Mozambique, Angola, or Portuguese Guinea may choose to be as friendly with Portugal as Brazil is. That would be the free choice of a free people.

16. In *Rhodesia* the situation is different in so far as the metro-politan power has acknowledged the colonial status of the territory. Unfortunately, however, it has failed to take ade-quate measures to re-assert its authority against the minority which has seized power with the declared intention of main-taining white domination. The matter cannot rest there.

Rhodesia, like the rest of Africa, must be free, and its independence must be on the basis of majority rule. If the
colonial power is unwilling or unable to effect such a transfer of power to the people, then the people themselves will
have no alternative but to capture it as and when they can.
And Africa has no alternative but to support them. The
question which remains in Rhodesia is therefore whether
Britain will re-assert her authority in Rhodesia and then
negotiate the peaceful progress to majority rule before independence. In so far as Britain is willing to make this second
commitment, Africa will co-operate in her attempts to re-
assert her authority. This is the method of progress which
we would prefer; it would involve less suffering for all the
people of Rhodesia, both black and white. But until there is
some firm evidence that Britain accepts the principle of independence on the basis of majority rule and is prepared to
take whatever steps are necessary to make it a reality, then
Africa has no choice but to support the struggle for the
people's freedom by whatever means are open.

17. Just as a settlement of the Rhodesian problem with a minimum of violence is a British responsibility, so a settlement
in *South-West Africa* with a minimum of violence is a United
Nations responsibility. By every canon of international law,
and by every precedent, South-West Africa should by now
have been a sovereign independent State with a government
based on majority rule. South-West Africa was a German
Colony until 1919, just as Tanganyika, Rwanda and Burundi,
Togoland, and Cameroon were German colonies.

It was a matter of European politics that when the Manda-
tory system was established after Germany had been defeated, the administration of South-West Africa was given
to the white minority government of South Africa, while the
other ex-German colonies in Africa were put into the hands
of the British, Belgian or French governments. After the
second world war every mandated territory except South-
West Africa was converted into a Trustee Territory and has
subsequently gained independence. South Africa, on the
other hand, has persistently refused to honour even the

international obligation it accepted in 1919, and has increasingly applied to South-West Africa the inhuman doctrines and organization of apartheid.

18. The United Nations General Assembly has ruled against this action and in 1966 terminated the Mandate under which South Africa had a legal basis for its occupation and domination of South-West Africa. The General Assembly declared that the territory is now the direct responsibility of the United Nations and set up an *ad hoc* committee to recommend practical means by which South-West Africa would be administered, and the people enabled to exercise self-determination and to achieve independence.

19. Nothing could be clearer than this decision – which no permanent member of the Security Council voted against. Yet, since that time, no effective measures have been taken to enforce it. South-West Africa remains in the clutches of the most ruthless minority government in Africa. Its people continue to be oppressed and those who advocate even peaceful progress to independence continue to be persecuted. The world has an obligation to use its strength to enforce the decision which all the countries co-operated in making. If they do this there is hope that the change can be effected without great violence. If they fail, then sooner or later the people of South-West Africa will take the law into their own hands. The people have been patient beyond belief, but one day their patience will be exhausted. Africa, at least, will then be unable to deny their call for help.

20. *The Republic of South Africa* is itself an independent sovereign state and a member of the United Nations. It is more highly developed and richer than any other nation in Africa. On every legal basis its internal legal affairs are a matter exclusively for the people of South Africa. Yet the purpose of law is people and we assert that the actions of the South African government are such that the rest of the world has a responsibility to take some action in defence of humanity.

21. There is one thing about South African oppression which distinguishes it from other oppressive regimes. The apartheid policy adopted by its government, and supported to a

greater or lesser extent by almost all its white citizens, is based on a rejection of man's humanity. A position of privilege or the experience of oppression in the South African society depends on the one thing which it is beyond the power of any man to change. It depends upon a man's colour, his parentage, and his ancestors. If you are black you cannot escape this categorization; nor can you escape it if you are white. If you are a black millionaire and a brilliant political scientist, you are still subject to the pass laws and still excluded from political activity. If you are white, even protests against the system and an attempt to reject segregation, will lead you only to the segregation and the comparative comfort of a white jail. Beliefs, abilities, and behaviour are all irrelevant to a man's status; everything depends upon race. Manhood is irrelevant. The whole system of government and society in South Africa is based on the denial of human equality. And the system is maintained by a ruthless denial of the human rights of the majority of the population and thus, inevitably, of all.

22. These things are known and are regularly condemned in the Councils of the United Nations and elsewhere. But it appears that to many countries international law takes precedence over humanity; therefore no action follows the words. Yet even if international law is held to exclude active assistance to the South African opponents of apartheid, it does not demand that the comfort and support of human and commercial intercourse should be given to a government which rejects the manhood of most of humanity. South Africa should be excluded from the United Nations Agencies, and even from the United Nations itself. It should be ostracized by the world community. It should be isolated from world trade patterns and left to be self-sufficient if it can. The South African government cannot be allowed both to reject the very concept of mankind's unity, and to benefit by the strength given through friendly international relations. And certainly Africa cannot acquiesce in the maintenance of the present policies against people of African descent.

23. The signatories of the Manifesto assert that the validity of the principles of human equality and dignity extend to the Republic of South Africa just as they extend to the colonial territories of Southern Africa. Before a basis for peaceful development can be established in this continent, these principles must be acknowledged by every nation, and in every State there must be a deliberate attempt to implement them.

24. We re-affirm our commitment to these principles of human equality and human dignity, and to the doctrines of self-determination and non-racialism. We shall work for their extension within our own nations and throughout the continent of Africa.

The conference was attended by the representatives of Ethiopa, Kenya, Rwanda, Malawi, Congo (Brazzaville), Congo (Kinshasa), Somalia, Burundi, Central African Republic, Sudan, Tanzania, Chad, Uganda and Zambia itself.

South-West Africa: SWAPO Leader's Statement

The following statement was made by Toivo Ja Toivo at the conclusion of the trial in Pretoria of himself and other members of the South-West Africa Peoples Organization. The circumstances are briefly described in the document. It is a moving expression of the mind of an African leader, as he is led to give moral and physical support to those who struggle for their human rights and national independence.

The trial opened first in August 1967 and ended in February 1968. Thirty of the accused were found guilty of terrorism. Three changed their pleas during the trial from Not Guilty to Guilty under the alternative charge of violating the Suppression of Communism Act and this was accepted by the prosecution. One was found not guilty, and one died from natural causes during the course of the trial.

Professor Richard Falk who attended part of the trial as an Observer for the I.C.J.[1] said that South African police have evidently made numerous arrests (estimates range from 100 to 250) since 1966 of South-West Africans accused of participating in or alleged to have information about guerilla activity in Ovamboland, South-West Africa. They have been detained incommunicado, in prisons evidently located in South Africa, often being held for many months without access to family or lawyer and without being charged or brought to trial. It is uncertain how many South Africans are presently detained in South African prisons on this basis. The defendants in the Pretoria Terrorist Trial were all held for long periods.

Mr Ja Toivo told the court that as South-West Africans he

[1] International Commission of Jurists.

and his fellow accused felt themselves to be in a foreign court in Pretoria where they had been tried by a Judge 'who is not our countryman and who has not shared our background'. He continued:

> We have always regarded South Africa as an intruder in our country . . . I speak of 'we' because I am trying to speak, not only for myself, but for others as well, and especially for those of my fellow accused who have not had the benefit of any education. I think also that when I say 'we' the overwhelming majority of non-white people in South-West Africa would like to be included. . . .
>
> The South African government has again shown its strength by detaining us for as long as it pleased; keeping some of us in solitary confinement for 300 to 400 days and bringing us to its capital to try us. . . . A Court can only do justice in political cases if it understands the position of those that it has in front of it. The State has not only wanted to convict us, but also to justify the policy of the South African government. We will not try to present the other side of the picture, because we know that a Court that has not suffered in the same way as we have, cannot understand us. This is perhaps why it is said that one should be tried by one's equals. We have felt from the very time of our arrest that we were not being tried by our equals but by our masters, and that those who have brought us to trial very often do not even do us the courtesy of calling us by our surnames. . . .

Of his party, the South-West African Peoples Organization, Mr Ja Toivo said:

> South African officials want to believe that SWAPO is an irresponsible organization and that it is an organization that resorts to the level of telling people not to get vaccinated. As much as white South Africans want to believe this, this is not SWAPO. We sometimes feel that it is what the government would like SWAPO to be. It may be true that some member or even members of SWAPO somewhere refused to do this. The reason for such a refusal is that some people in our part

of the world have lost confidence in the governors of our country, and they are not prepared to accept even the good they are trying to do.

Your government, my Lord, undertook a very special responsibility when it was awarded the mandate over us after the first world war. It assumed a sacred trust to guide us towards independence and to prepare us to take our place among the nations of the world. We believe that South Africa has abused that trust because of its belief in racial supremacy . . . and apartheid. We believe that for fifty years South Africa has failed to promote the development of our people. Where are our trained men? The wealth of our country has been used to train your people for leadership and the sacred duty of preparing the indigenous people to take their place among the nations of the world has been ignored.

I know of no case in the last twenty years of a parent who did not want his child to go to school if the facilities were available, but even if, as it was said, a small percentage of parents want their children to look after cattle, I am sure that South Africa was strong enough to impose its will on this as it has done in so many other respects. To us it has always seemed that our rulers wanted to keep us backward for their benefit.

1963 was for us to be the year of our freedom. From 1960 it looked as if South Africa could not oppose the world for ever. The world is important to us. In the same way as all laughed in court when they heard that an old man tried to bring down a helicopter with a bow and arrow, we laughed when South Africa said that it would oppose the world. We knew that the world was divided, but as time went on it at least agreed that South Africa had no right to rule us.

I do not claim that it is easy for men of different races to live at peace with one another. I myself had no experience of this in my youth, and at first it surprised me that men of different races could live together in peace. But now I know it to be true and to be something for which we must strive. . . .

I have come to know that our people cannot expect progress as a gift from anyone, be it the United Nations or South Africa. Progress is something we shall have to struggle and work for.

And I believe that the only way in which we shall be able and fit to secure that progress is to learn from our own experience and mistakes.

Your Lordship emphasized in your judgment the fact that our arms came from communist countries, and also that words commonly used by communists were to be found in our documents. . . . Many documents finish up with an appeal to the Almighty to guide us in our struggle for freedom. It is the wish of the South African government that we should be discredited in the Western world. That is why it calls our struggle a communist plot; but this will not be believed by the world . . .

Mr Ja Toivo spoke of the bitter disappointment over the judgment of the World Court.

We felt betrayed and we believed that South Africa would never fulfil its trust. Some felt that we could secure our freedom only by fighting for it. We know that the power of South Africa is overwhelming, but we also know that our case is a just one and our situation intolerable – why should we not also receive our freedom? We are sure that the world's efforts to help us in our plight will continue, whatever South Africans may call us.

We do not expect that independence will end our troubles, but we do believe that our people are entitled – as are all people – to rule themselves. It is not really a question of whether South Africa treats us well or badly, but that South-West Africa is our country and we wish to be our own masters.

There are some who will say that they are sympathetic with our aims, but that they condemn violence. I would answer that I am not by nature a man of violence and I believe that violence is a sin against God and my fellow men. SWAPO itself was a non-violent organization, but the South African government is not truly interested in whether opposition is violent or non-violent. It does not wish to hear any opposition to apartheid. Since 1963 SWAPO meetings have been banned. It is true that it is the tribal authorities who have done so, but they work with the South African government, which has never lifted a finger in favour of political freedom. We have found ourselves voteless in our own country and deprived of the right to meet and state our political opinions.

Is it surprising that in such times my countrymen have taken up arms? Violence is truly fearsome, but who would not defend himself and his property against a robber? And we believe that South Africa has robbed us of our country. . . .

In 1964 the ANC and the PAC in South Africa were suppressed. This convinced me that we were too weak to face South Africa's force by waging battle. When some of my country's soldiers came back I foresaw the trouble there would be for SWAPO, my people and me personally; I tried to do what I could to prevent my people going into the bush. In my attempts I became unpopular with some of my people, but this too I was prepared to endure. Decisions of this kind are not easy to make. My loyalty is to my country. My organization could not work properly – it could not even hold meetings. I had no answer to the question 'Where has your non-violence got us?' Whilst the World Court judgment was pending, I at least had that to fall back on. When we failed after years of waiting I had no answer to give to my people.

Even though I did not agree that people should go into the bush I could not refuse to help them when I knew that they were hungry. I even passed on the request for dynamite. It was not an easy decision. I was not and I could not remain a spectator in the struggle of my people for their freedom . . .

Mr Ja Toivo concluded:

My co-accused and I have suffered. We are not looking forward to our imprisonment. We do not, however, feel that our efforts and sacrifice have been wasted. We believe that human suffering has its effect even on those who impose it. We hope that what has happened will persuade the Whites of South Africa that we and the world may be right and they may be wrong. Only when White South Africans realize this and act on it will it be possible for us to stop our struggle for freedom and justice in the land of our birth.

Quotations from Reports at WCC Assembly, Uppsala 1968:
Uppsala 68 Speaks

Page 31 para (b). Revolutionary movements

The longing for a just society is causing revolutions all over the world. Since many Christians are deeply rooted in the *status quo* they tend to be primarily concerned for the maintenance of law and order. Where the maintenance of order is an obstacle to a just order, some will decide for revolutionary action against that injustice, struggling for a just society without which the new humanity cannot fully come. The Christian community must decide whether it can recognize the validity of their decision and support them.

Page 32 para 3. How to find criteria for missionary priorities

Because the world is always changing, it is always necessary to evaluate missionary priorities. That evaluation will often require willingness to face loss in prestige and finance, and detachment from monuments of faithfulness in mission localities of the past. We suggest the following criteria for such evaluation :

do they place the church alongside the poor, the defenceless, the abused, the forgotten, the bored?

do they allow Christians to enter the concerns of others to accept their issues and their structures as vehicles of involvement?

are they the best situations for discerning with other men the signs of the times, and for moving with history towards the coming of the new humanity?

Page 45 para 4. The Christian Concern for Development

Our hope is in him who makes all things new. He judges our structures of thought and action, and renders them obsolete. If our false security in the old and our fear of revolutionary change tempt us to defend the *status quo* or to patch it up with half-hearted measures, we may all perish. The death of the old may cause pain to some, but failure to build up a new world community may bring death to all. In their faith in the coming Kingdom of God and in their search for his righteousness, Christians are urged to participate in the struggle of millions of people for greater social justice and for world development.

Page 49–50 paras 22 and 23. Discrimination

In the struggle of oppressed people for economic justice, white racism is often an aggressive force which impedes and distorts development. Feelings of superiority among white people – a critical area of spiritual sickness and underdevelopment – diminish their humanity, and make them unable to engage in meaningful encounter with persons of different colour. Racism as it has become institutionalized in political, educational and economic systems, brutalizes and destroys those who suffer discrimination and prevents them from reaching their full potential as persons, citizens and participants in the economy. In many parts of the world, development has also increased the self-consciousness of religious, ethnic and tribal groups, leading to discrimination and conflicts. Discrimination against women is another pervasive impediment to personal and community development.

The church must actively promote the redistribution of power, without discrimination of any kind, so that all men, women and young people may participate in the benefits of development.

Page 53 para 39. The Political Task

Many of the foregoing tasks are especially appropriate for churches in development countries. Churches in developing countries should:

1. integrate their social and educational services in a concerted effort to awaken the conscience of people to the realities of the existing situation, and reflect this concern in their normal worship activities;
2. make the cause of the disinherited their own, giving voice to the masses;
3. take an open and public position calling on their communities to realize the need for revolutionary change.

Page 65 para 28. Race Relations

Contemporary racism robs all human rights of their meaning, and is an imminent danger to world peace. The crucial nature of the present situation is emphasized by the official policies of certain governments, racial violence in many countries, and the racial component in the gap between rich and poor nations. Only immediate action directed to root causes can avoid widespread violence or war.

Page 66 para (a). Race Relations

Racism is linked with economic, and political exploitation. The churches must be actively concerned for the economic and political well-being of exploited groups so that their statements and actions may be relevant. In order that victims of racism may regain a sense of their own worth and be enabled to determine their own future, the churches must make economic and educational resources available to underprivileged groups for their development to full participation in the social and economic life of their communities. They should also withdraw investments from institutions that perpetuate racism. They must also urge that similar assistance be given from both the public and private sectors. Such economic help is an essential compensatory measure to counteract and overcome the present systematic exclusion of victims of racism from the main stream of economic life. The churches must also work for the change of those political processes which prevent the victims of racism from participating fully in the civic and governmental structures of their countries.

Page 67 para 31. Economic Justice and World Order

A fuller treatment of world economic justice lies with Section III. Section IV must consider the relationship between economic justice and world order. The increasing economic gap between the affluent minority and the vast majority of underprivileged peoples of the world emphasizes the urgency of the need to deal more effectively with world economic justice. It is now clear that poverty, racism and violence conjoin to perpetuate the economic and political injustice which today bring suffering to millions of people in many areas of the world. Unless the relative rate of growth of the developing countries is increased substantially by vigorous international action, it seems certain that outbreaks of disorder will proliferate on an international scale. Some Christians will be among those who, despairing of the removal or reduction of economic injustice by peaceful means, feel obliged to have recourse to violence as a last resort. In such circumstances, both violent action and passive inaction come under God's judgment. Since recourse to violence could end in a defeat for both justice and order, special attention should be paid to non-violent strategies for the achievement of change.

Page 68 para 34. Economic Justice and World Order
To enable the churches to play their rightful role in the struggle for world economic justice, it is imperative that they:

(a) Express in their own life the truth that all men are created equal in God's sight, and share a common humanity. In particular, they must move beyond the piece-meal and paternalistic programmes of charity which have sometimes characterised Christian missions and must confront positively the systematic injustice of the world economy.

(b) Strive more actively and urgently for that reform of will and conscience among the people of the world which alone can inspire the achievement of greater international justice. To this end, the churches should particularly concern themselves with political parties, trades unions and other groups influencing public opinion. They should also stress that economic justice cannot be achieved without sacrifice and support the establishment of an international development tax.

(c) Give greater priority and more money to ministries of reconciliation and service on an international scale, and especially where the most explosive forms of injustice are to be found.

(d) Pursue studies of the root causes of violence in our societies with a view to their removal and also of non-violent strategies of revolution and social change.

Bibliography

GENERAL

Christian Social Ethics in a Changing World, ed. J. C. Bennett, SCM Press, 1966.
Race Relations in Portuguese Colonial Empire, 1415–1825, C. R. Boxer, OUP, 1963.
The Death of Africa, H. Y. P. Ritner, Macmillan, 1960.
The African Awakening, B. Davidson, Cape, 1955.
The City of God and the Politics of Crisis, E. Brookes, OUP, 1960.
The Roots of Guerilla Warfare, Douglas Hyde, Bodley Head, 1968.
The Just War in Revolutionary Situations, Paul Ramsey (USA).
The Language of Christian Revolution, N. Middleton, Sheed and Ward, 1968.
Which Way Africa?, B. Davidson, Penguin, 1967.
The Pacifist Conscience, ed. P. Mayer, Penguin, 1966.
The Race War, R. Segal, Cape, 1966.
The Wretched of the Earth, F. Fanon, Penguin, 1967.
Persecution, P. Benenson, Penguin.
What Kind of Revolution?, James Klugmann and Paul Oestreicher, Panther, 1968.
Terrorism in Southern Africa, M. Horrell, Institute of Race Relations, 1968.
Unyoung, Uncoloured, Unpoor, Colin Morris, Epworth Press, 1969.
Africa Handbook, Penguin Reference Books, 1969.
Southern Africa. A Time For Change, Friendship Press (USA), 1969.
Race and Politics in Africa, J. V. Taylor, Penguin.
Violence, Jacques Ellul, SCM Press, 1970.
Industrialization and Race Relations. A Symposium, ed. G. Hunter, OUP for IRR, 1965.

UN Documents on South Africa are available at UN Association main offices.

RHODESIA

The Origins of Rhodesia, Stanlake Samkange, Heinemann Educ., 1969.
The Character and Legislation of the Rhodesia Front Since UDI, Reg Austin, Africa Bureau, 1968.
The Road to Rebellion, James Barber, IRR/OUP, 1967.
Revolt in Southern Rhodesia 1896–7, T. O. Ranger, Heinemann Educ., 1967
African Nationalism, N. Sithole, OUP, 1968.
The High Price of Principles, Richard Hall, Hodder & Stoughton.
Rhodesia: The Course to Collision, Frank Clements, Pall Mall, 1969.
Let Tangwena Be, Guy Clutton-Brock, Mambo Press, 1969.
Christianity and Separate Development, C. W. Alderson and others, Mambo Press, 1967.
Aspects of Rhodesia Land Policy 1890–1936, R. H. Palmer, Salisbury, 1968.
Rhodesian Perspective, Theodore Bull, Michael Joseph, 1967.
Crisis in Rhodesia, Nathan Shamuyarira, Deutsch, 1965.
The Price of Freedom, Bulawayo, 1964.
The Birth of a Dilemma, Philip Mason, IRR/OUP, 1958.
Year of Decision, Philip Mason, IRR/OUP, 1960.
A Principle in Torment – The UN and Rhodesia, UN, 1969.
Politics of Partnership, Patrick Keatley, Penguin, 1963.

SOUTH AFRICA

The Violence of Apartheid, A. Sachs, Christian Action, 1969.
The Peasant's Revolt, G. Mbeki, Penguin, 1964.
The Sharpeville Incident and its International Significance, UN, 1968, ST/PSCA/SERA/5.
The Rise of the South African Reich, B. Bunting, 2nd ed., Penguin, 1970.
Class and Colour in South Africa, 1850–1950, H. J. Simons and R. E. Simon, Penguin, 1969.
African Opposition in South Africa: The Failure of Passive Resistance, Hoover Institution.

South Africa: Crisis for the West, Colin and Margaret Legum, Pall Mall, 1964.
The Future of South Africa, The British Council of Churches, SCM Press, 1965.
Bantustans, C. R. Hill, IRR/OUP.
South Africa: The Struggle for a Birthright, Mary Benson, Penguin, 1966.
Verwoerd, Alex Hepple, Penguin, 1967.
Sanctions Against South Africa, ed. R. Segal, Penguin.
The Oxford History of South Africa, Vol. One, OUP, 1969; Vol. Two, OUP, 1970.
A Plea for Understanding, W. A. Landman.
The Church in South Africa, Peter Hinchliff, SPCK, 1968.
Erosion of the Rule of Law in South Africa, International Commission of Jurists, 1968.
Let My People Go, A. J. Luthuli, Collins: Fontana, 1963.
The Discarded People, C. Desmond, The Christian Institute, 1970.
The South African Economy, D. H. Houghton, OUP, 1964.

SOUTH-WEST AFRICA

A Time to Speak, Michael Scott, Faber, 1958.
South-West Africa, Ruth First, Penguin.
UN General Assembly, A/6700/October 31st, 1967.
South-West Africa, Muriel Horrell, SAIRR, 1967.

PORTUGUESE TERRITORIES

The Ovimbundu Under Two Sovereignties, A. C. Edwards, OUP, 1962.
Portugal's African Wards, Martin Harris, New York, 1968.
Angola Awake, Gilchrist, The Riverson Press, 1968.
Cry Angola!, L. Addicott, SCM Press, 1962.
Angola in Flames, K. M. Panikkar, Asia Publicity House, 1962.
Angola: A Symposium –Views of a Revolt, OUP, 1962.
The Struggle for Mozambique, E. Mondlane, Penguin, 1969.
Portugal in Africa, James Duffy, Penguin.
A Principle in Torment, II: The UN and the Portuguese Territories, UN, 1970.
The Portuguese Conquest of Angola, D. Birmingham, IRR/OUP, 1965.

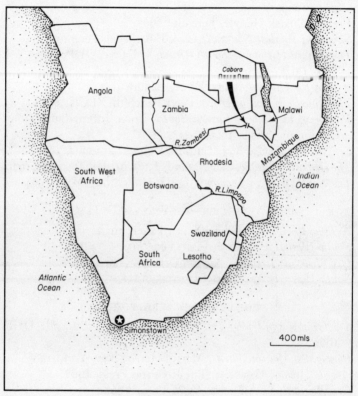

Southern Africa